Pirouettes on the Prairie

ERIC BERGESON

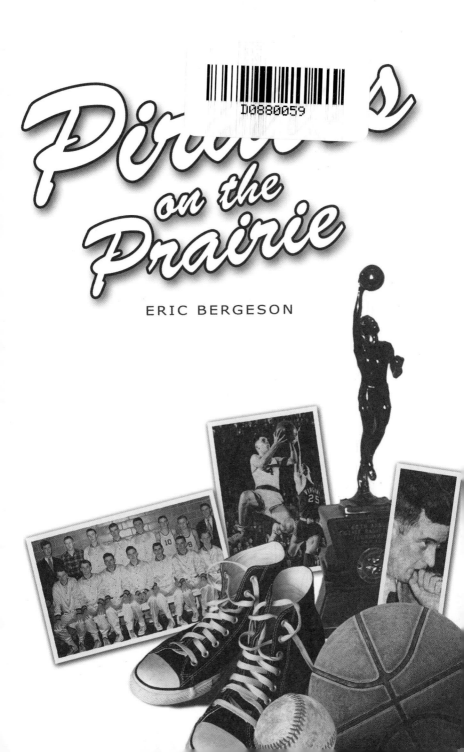

MYERS HOUSE

Myers House LLC
813 56th Street
West Des Moines, IA 50266
ISBN: 0-9721900-2-3

To order additional copies of this book:

Phone: 515-278-1292
Orders: 1-800-278-1292
Fax: 515-270-0694
E-Mail: info@piratesontheprairie.com
Website: http://www.piratesontheprairie.com

Table of Contents

Foreword

Pirates on the Prairie has been a three-year adventure for me. The people I have met and the stories I have heard have all contributed to an incredible journey. During this process I have been asked a number of times, "Why are you doing this?" My answer has always been, "It is something I have wanted to do for a long, long time."

Even though I moved to Iowa 45 years ago, my ties to the town of Halstad have remained strong and enduring. I was born in a hospital located in the center of Halstad (population 590). I grew up nearby on a 400-acre farm, now designated a "Century Farm," that is still in our family today. I developed so many wonderful friendships in Halstad, friendships that are still part of my life.

The impetus for this book was the significant impact the events and players back in 1952 had on me and the Halstad community. I was a mere fifth grader when this group of guys took the entire Halstad area on a memorable ride that was as much a dream as an actual experience. In 1952 expectations for success had been building for a couple of years. We followed every basketball game either in person or on the radio. (Remember, we did not have television back then.) My grade school friends and I viewed

"The '52 Team" with awe and adulation. Seeing one of them in the hallway was cause to stand back and stare. Seeing Ted Williams or Mickey Mantle would have been no more exciting than seeing a member of "The '52 Team" casually meandering down the street.

The larger-than-life image created by these five guys was not only about their success in sports. They all had a confident dignity about them that made them even bigger heroes to a young grade-schooler. Fifty-five years later, when I became re-acquainted with The Starting Five, they still possessed that same quality of control and self-confidence. It is no wonder they had such an impact upon me back in the early '50s.

For years I thought the exploits of Akason, Hesby, Holm, Serum, and Thompson should be chronicled. However, I never carried it any further. Then, I began noticing Eric Bergeson's newspaper columns and a light went on. Here is a guy who writes beautifully, and better yet, he is from small-town in northern Minnesota. He would be perfect to write the book!

Eric and I agreed from the start that *Pirates on the Prairie* would be more than a sports story. It would be a book that captured the culture of northern Minnesota at the time—including the history and uniqueness of the little town of Halstad. It would be a book that looked into the lives of the players and the coaches to answer these questions:

- Where did these young men come from?
- What influenced them?
- How did they develop into such an outstanding team?

Eric did a masterful job of researching, reading, and conducting interviews with people to explore and convey the answers to our questions. He has retold this story in the good-humored, subdued, rhythmic voice that is his trademark.

Pirates on the Prairie would never have happened without the support of my wife, Barbara. When obstacles presented themselves, she encouraged me to go ahead with a life-long dream, and she provided me with many helpful ideas along the way. Lori DeLong, who lives in Halstad, helped me every time a photo was needed or a page had to be turned. Kathy Myers, the publisher, generously guided me with her expertise and creativity. I also appreciate the assistance of Ron Laqua, Amy Hoey, and Erika Stennes. These people and countless others turned this childhood experience into an adult adventure.

Clarence Stennes, February, 2008

Foreword

My first thoughts after finishing a very enjoyable few hours reading this book were that it could have been titled, *A Little Boy's Heroes*; *The Rise and Decline of a Small Town*; or *A Nostalgic Journey*. I was born and lived in a small farm-service village in southern Minnesota. After graduating from country school, I rode the first bus in the community that transported students to high school in Owatonna, Minnesota.

While reading the story I thought back to my days when we country students occasionally were referred to as a "dumb farmer," "plow jockey," "hayseed," or "hick" by the big-time city kids, an experience had by many others during the transition years from the late 1920s to the 1950s, after which the country schools basically disappeared from the scene. This was a strong theme that author Eric Bergeson used throughout the story. Bergeson, a very successful nurseryman in the Red River Valley area, uses his writing talents to provide weekly columns for area newspapers, making him an excellent choice to write this account, for he was aware of the transition. In some respects the story seems to be a fantasy cleverly woven into a socio-economic and cultural history of what was happening in agriculture and small towns throughout rural America.

When Norwegian immigrants of the 1870s were squeezed out of Scandinavian communities in Wisconsin and Iowa because most of the available farmland there was already settled, they moved to the frontier of the Red River Valley of the North. Soon this choice land was occupied with a farm on each quarter section while others settled in Halstad and established businesses, churches, and schools to serve the farmers. The Great Northern Railroad came through the area, and soon Halstad grew to a thriving village of 500 residents and remained at that figure for decades to come.

The Halstad school population remained static because initially it served only children of the residents and a limited number of farm girls who wanted to further their education. The girls usually worked to pay for their board and room with people in the village. Few boys went to high school because they were needed on the farm.

In the 1920s, farms started to mechanize, and their numbers began a prolonged decline, a trend that has continued. As the rural population decreased, the country schools closed, and the districts consolidated with the closest town school. The Halstad school population increased with the influx of rural boys and girls. During World War II, a second farm prosperity gave a second short-lived spurt to business on Main Street. It was during this period that the story took place—a story about a small community whose high school athletes earned their way to two state tournaments where they achieved third place in basketball and first place in baseball. In each case they faced teams from Austin, the largest high school in Minnesota at the time.

Five adults set the stage for Halstad's brief claim to regional fame. The Reverend Carl Opsahl was called to a three-point parish in the 1940s, and, aided by his wife, Olina, worked hard to set a positive moral tone for the community's youth in the rapidly changing society. The Opsahls were backed by the community women whose task it was to provide abundant feasts at the local events that made up much of the social life in the area.

In 1946 Arnold Kittleson became superintendent of the school. His tight fiscal management served the school and the community well.

In 1948 Ray Kerrigan, whose service in the Air Force had taught him discipline and motivational skills, was hired as principal and teacher. He had taken part in music instead of sports in college, but because no one else was qualified to do the job, he was assigned to coach Halstad's baseball, basketball, and football.

In 1950 Larry MacLeod, who had been an excellent

student and star athlete in college, joined the faculty as a history teacher and assistant coach. He, too, loved working with youth and, like Kerrigan, was a disciplinarian. They became a good team.

The above were joined by Erwin Warner, a local farmer whose behavior was not a role model for youth. He made athletics his hobby which worked to the detriment of his farm business.

These key people blended the city boys with the "farm kids" to make 1952 the banner year in the history of Halstad. The achievements of a small number of highly motivated and team-centered athletes united the residents with a sense of community spirit and pride. That is what makes the story unique. Bergeson has done a splendid job weaving these events into a free-flowing, interesting, and enjoyable read.

Accolades go to Clarence Stennes who made his heroes from his fifth-grade memories come to life by providing the means to record part of his home town history for future generations to enjoy. He collected material for a half century to make this fine addition to Americana possible.

Hiram M. Drache,
Concordia College,
Moorhead, Minnesota

Acknowledgements

This book would not have been written but for the determination of Clarence Stennes, who, in addition to serving as the publisher, supported the research and writing at every step. For all that I learned on this project and for all of the wonderful people I met while researching it, I am thankful to Clarence.

Thanks to the Starting Five and their spouses—Jim and Carol Akason, Darrel and Janet Hesby, Don and Jane Thompson, Morrie and Maxine Holm and Dale and Carol Serum—for welcoming me into their homes for lengthy interviews, for gallons of coffee, and for giving me complete access to their scrapbooks and mementos.

Thanks to Roger Williamson for his hours of time, useful insights and good stories.

Thanks to Gene Thompson for the guided tour of historic Halstad and Little Chicago.

Thanks to Wally Oien and Roger Stole for a delightful afternoon of detailed and valuable reminiscences.

Thanks to the Kerrigan sisters, Kristi Phillipay and Karen Pitsenbarger, for sharing memories of their beloved father Ray.

Thanks to Larry Macleod for sharing his memories of Halstad and his career there.

Thanks to Paul Opsahl for his insightful observations about his father, Rev. Carl Opsahl.

Thanks to Audrey and Melissa at the Ada Public Library for their kind help.

Thanks to Marlyn Aanenson, Don Lervold, Franklyn Steenerson, Professor George "Squirt" Johnson, Curt Johnson, Rod Oistad, Bucky Wang, Paul and Rita Viker, Jack Nelson, John Conzemius, Allen Williamson, Bruce Williamson, Don Rasmussen, Harris Henderson, Erman Ueland, and Dick Nielson for submitting to interviews, some lengthy, some brief, but every one of which added to the book.

Thank you to Chester Mauritson, Dorothy Steen, Gene Thompson, and Jeanette Enger for their stories and useful background information.

Thank you to Lori DeLong for her assistance.

And a special thanks to the compilers of the Halstad Centennial Book, published in 1983. It contains a treasure trove of historical information.

Eric Bergeson
June, 2008

Chapter 1

Meeting the Starting Five

July 17, 2005. The calendar read that I was to be in Halstad, Minnesota, at 1 p.m., where I would interview the Starting Five of the Halstad Pirates basketball team of 1952. The men, now in their early seventies, were back in Halstad for an all-school reunion held at Norman County West High School, formerly the home of Halstad High.

The meeting was the result of a phone call a couple of months earlier from Clarence Stennes, a former resident of Halstad. I wasn't expected to know him, Clarence said, but he had read some of my newspaper articles and thought that I might be interested in a project he had in mind.

Clarence is a retired lawyer and businessman now living in Des Moines, Iowa. But in 1952, when Clarence was in fifth grade in Halstad, the Halstad Pirates basketball team finished third in the state of Minnesota. A few months later, the same athletes, give or take one or two, won the state baseball title. Clarence had always thought that the story should be written up. He didn't ask that I commit to the project, only that I spend one afternoon with the players.

I agreed, but with little hope that the meeting would amount to much. Small town teams that nearly win state titles are a dime a dozen, especially now that schools are divided into so many classes that a trip to the state tournament is almost an entitlement. As an alumnus of Fertile-Beltrami High School, forty miles to Halstad's northeast, I recall with civic pride our second place finish in wrestling in 1977, our second place finish in baseball in 1979, and our second place finish to Minneapolis North in basketball in 1996. If I were going to research the long-forgotten exploits of aging athletes, I had more than enough material on my home turf.

That didn't mean I couldn't enjoy the drive across the prairie on a beautiful July afternoon. The flat farmlands of Northwestern Minnesota are a barren waste in winter, but if you're there in mid-July, the prairie is endlessly rich with green crops about to ripen. Beets, soybeans, and wheat stretch across half-mile-long fields in rows made eerily straight by Global Positioning System steering devices on the tractors. The relentless green rows can hypnotize a driver, especially on a still day in mid-July, that short respite at the peak of summer before the Minnesota seasons descend with gathering speed towards harvest, autumn, and the dark depths of winter.

Halstad sits in the very middle of the enormous Red

River Valley of the North, the lakebed of ancient Lake Agassiz, a rich flatland of black soil. "Valley" is an odd name for what appears to be relentless prairie. The great agricultural valleys of California are flat, but they are flanked by mountain ranges that give one the sense of being in a valley. Not so with Lake Agassiz's floor. The Red River Valley is so flat that some newcomers complain of feeling as if they are being pressed against the sky.

The Valley runs seven hundred miles from north to south and up to one hundred miles from east to west. It is bordered by low sandhills, the ancient beaches that rise so gently that non-prairie dwellers usually don't even notice. The Valley is split down the middle by the Red River, a meandering, muddy estuary that curls its way north in tight curly-cues. The river's twists and turns form a border between the Dakotas and Minnesota, which looks, if you view it on a national map, deceptively straight.

The Red River is usually well-behaved, even sleepy, a barely noticed feature of life on the prairie. Once every decade or so, however, it goes on a rip-roaring drunk. Fueled by snowmelt, the river jumps its banks and fans out across the flat prairie like a glass of chocolate milk spilled across the kitchen table. Once out of its banks, for every foot the water rises, the river widens by one mile. The floods generate about the only national attention to come to the Red River Valley, which is otherwise a blank spot on the nation's consciousness.

Residents of the Red River Valley might point out that fifteen percent of the nation's sugar is grown in the form of beets in the Red River Valley's black, gumbo soil. They also might tell you that the Red River Valley was once known as the "breadbasket of the world" due to its leadership in wheat production.

But Red River Valley residents are pretty humble. Although the Red River Valley still raises bumper crops, the population of its rural areas has been reduced to a tiny fraction of what it once was by the relentless expansion of farms. Where the average farm was once 200 acres, today farms of 15,000 acres are common. With the loss of the rural population has come a decline and loss of institutions such as churches, schools, clubs, and Main Street businesses. With those losses in community life has come a sense that the future is elsewhere. Since 1920 when the Red River Valley's countryside population was at its peak, the area has exported not only crops but people by the thousands.

Thus, the "bread basket of the world" hoopla of one hundred years ago, designed to draw even more immigrants to the Valley, has slowly given way to a tired resignation to cold economic facts. The solid Scandinavian descendants of the sturdy immigrants who settled the area have learned to neither brag nor complain. Decay and decline are a way of life. A person can get used to it or do what a good share of those born in the Red River Valley have done over the past century: leave for greener pastures.

Clarence had laid out a schedule. I was to appear at his mother Cora's apartment at 1 p.m. I would spend an hour looking through scrapbooks of clippings from the 1952 season, books he had already collected from the players. I was to mark the articles I wanted copied. An hour later, a young man hired for the purpose would arrive and take the scrapbooks over to the local bank, which would be opened up, even though it was Saturday, to copy the clippings. The Starting Five would then arrive at Cora's apartment. I was to interview them for an hour. At that time, a professional photographer would take pictures. While the photographer did his thing, I would leave Cora Stennes' apartment and drive over to the meeting room at the phone company headquarters where I would meet the reserves on the 1952 basketball team, some of their wives, who were also the cheerleaders, and a few baseball players, all of whom were to be there waiting.

I arrived at Cora Stennes' apartment and met Clarence. The stack of scrapbooks sat on a table in the living room. Next to them was a ream of sticky pads I was to use to mark the clippings for copying. Clarence offered me a drink from several varieties of soda. He assumed, he said, that I didn't want anything stronger. He then departed for a school reunion activity, leaving me alone to read through clippings.

The crisp, musty, fifty-year-old newspaper clippings crumbled easily, as did the yellowed scrapbooks which held them. Yet nothing makes an hour go faster for a history buff like myself than a stack of musty newspaper clippings. I stared into the old pictures, tried to read the faces, studied the clothes, the uniforms, the glasses, the shoes, and the stilted language of the captions. The faces stared back at me from the musty, yellowed past.

Headlines in the *Minneapolis Star*, the *Minneapolis Tribune* and the *Fargo Forum* trumpeted the story of the underdog team from the tiny town on the prairie. Corny, staged pictures showed team members in the Curtis Hotel in Minneapolis gazing at television for the first time. Halstad reserve Marlyn Aanenson stood alone in the middle of the University of Minnesota's gigantic old basketball barn, Williams Arena. He was quoted as saying "This place would sure hold a lot of hay!" Center Don Thompson was pictured with his horse, Guard Morrie Holm with a sheep, Aanenson with his dog. The big city papers milked for all it was worth the story of the farm boys gone to the Big City.

I marked clippings by the dozen. As I got to the bottom of the stack of scrapbooks, the clippings began to repeat themselves. By then, I had become familiar with the names Kerrigan, Macleod, Hesby, Akason, Serum, Holm, and Thompson.

Through all of the articles and clippings, what most jumped off the page was the effervescent charisma of Coach Ray Kerrigan. His all-American smile, his intense glare, and his unmanaged shock of curly hair all stood out, as did his literate, sometimes inflated responses to reporters' questions.

"It is one of the great principles of the American democracy," he said after a Halstad victory over a favored foe, "that the people pull for the underdog." Indeed.

A knock on the door interrupted my thoughts. A young man entered as scheduled and carted the stack of scrapbooks off to the bank. I hoped that the crumbling paper would survive the ordeal of being pressed against the copier's glass.

Clarence returned, and one by one the Starting Five filtered into Cora's apartment. Far from the jovial, aging, pot-bellied jocks I expected, the five players were dignified, almost imposing. They settled into chairs, fanned out in a semi-circle in the living room, and patiently waited for the meeting to begin. There was very little small talk. I sat in the middle at my table as the inquisitor. Clarence started his video camera rolling and brought the meeting to order.

A successful lawyer and entrepreneur by trade, Clarence sounded more like an old-time gentleman Lutheran minister than a veteran of the corporate board-room. He clasped his hands in a formal manner. His every sentence, like the meeting itself, seemed meticulously planned. He finished each phrase with his gaze fixed on somebody in the room, eyebrows raised as if to drive home the point.

"Fifty years ago, if I had known I would be meeting with you five, I wouldn't have slept for two nights!" Clarence began, leaving the impression that the passage of time hadn't done much to improve matters. Looking in my direction, he said, slowly, relishing every syllable, "These guys walked on water."

I was beginning to understand. The Starting Five sat in dignified silence through Clarence's introduction, hands on their knees, eyes fixed in the distance as if this wasn't their first press conference. The mood in the room was less like a small-town cafe and more like old-timers day at Cooperstown.

I matched the boys pictured in old newspapers with the seventy-year-olds sitting before me in Cora Stennes' living room. It wasn't difficult. Morrie Holm's eyes were still ice blue. Catcher Dale Serum's ears still looked a bit like those of a certain Yankee catcher, thus, perhaps, his nickname, "Yogi." The years had transformed Jimmy Akason's square-jawed, movie-star looks into a senatorial dignity. Center Don Thompson was still lithe and lanky, his expression as innocent and guileless as it was in the clippings. Fidgety Darrel Hesby, disparaged by a rival town's newspaper fifty-five years ago as a "bespectacled little tow-head," was still bespectacled, still slight, still sporting a full head of brown hair without a hint of gray.

The interview started nervously for me. I asked a few general questions and finally hit one that sparked the men's interest. I asked about their coach, Ray Kerrigan. The respect and affection the men felt for him immediately showed.

"He was a master motivator," said Dale Serum. "He just made you feel you could do it."

"I think we all agree," Jim Akason said, "that Ray wasn't an Xs and Os man." In other words, he didn't know that much about basketball. But he knew human nature, and he knew how to get the most out of every player.

So where did the players learn their basketball? They played on their own from an early age. They developed their own rhythm. To practice, they snuck into the gym through the coal chute, or they propped a back door open during school hours and came back Saturday morning.

I asked about the men's fathers. "Were they in favor of your playing ball all the time? Did they show up for the games? Did they drive you to town for practice?"

The question brought a less immediate response than did the one on Kerrigan. The fathers were generally too busy making a living to worry much about sports, it seemed. Dale Serum's father, Orlando, was a carpenter who worked a dozen hours a day. Morrie Holm's father, Palmer, was a farmer attempting to make enough money from his 350-acre farm to feed his eleven children. Darrel Hesby's father, Allen, was the local bulk fuel dealer. Don Thompson's father, Leonard, worked for area farmers to support his wife and five children. None of these fathers stood in the way of their son's sports activities, but none of them seemed particularly involved, either. They just didn't have the time.

Only Martin Akason, father to Jimmy Akason, stood out as playing a role in his son's sports career. Martin Akason put up a basket in his driveway for Jimmy and his friends, probably the first outdoor basket put up in Halstad. And Martin made sure that Jimmy made an annual trip to Williams Arena in Minneapolis to see the biggest sporting event on the Minnesota sporting calendar at the time, the Boys State Basketball Tournament.

Talk drifted into the season of 1952, when the Starting Five nearly took the Minnesota State Basketball crown and when the Starting Nine later won the state baseball title. One story led to another and the hour disappeared quickly.

At the end of the hour, the copy boy returned from the bank, as scheduled, with scrapbooks to return to the Starting Five and a stack of copies for me to take home. In marched the professional photographer who had driven forty miles from Moorhead, Minnesota. He was followed by two assistants. The players posed in several combinations before they collected their scrapbooks and left for the meal at the school.

Later, I found out that the photographer, Dave Grosz, a city boy from Moorhead, Minnesota, remembered well the 1952 Halstad team, right down to the names of the

Starting Five. He was honored just to meet them, let alone to take their photos. I took note.

After meeting the Starting Five and reading the clippings, I got the feeling that if Halstad had a Mt. Rushmore, these men would be on it. With only one player who reached six feet in height and without a coach who knew much about basketball, they overwhelmed the northwest corner of Minnesota and eventually charmed the sporting audience of the entire state. Their magical run on the court ended in March of 1952, but once the snow melted, the same boys picked up their bats and gloves and began a new streak on the baseball diamond that cemented their status as small-town legends.

I headed off to the phone-company meeting room. About a dozen people were there, and I was introduced to all of them. However, I didn't know enough about the teams or the players from simply reading the clippings to ask intelligent questions of them. So they all wrote down their addresses and phone numbers, in case I should want to talk to them again, and we dispersed.

With the meetings over, Clarence took me to the all-school reunion dinner at the school. The organizers were expecting to serve up to 1,000. The dinner line wound through the hallways of Norman County West High School.

As usually happens with small town reunions, the bulk of the work is done by the minority who still live in town. Motivated by civic pride, they make the meals, organize the events, and spiff up the town. The expatriates return for the reunion, more than doubling the town's population. They eat the food, hobnob with classmates and old friends who also have come back from the city, and leave Sunday afternoon. The locals, too busy mashing potatoes to visit, wonder what hit them and resolve never to do it again. Of course, five years later, it happens all over.

At this school-reunion dinner, the locals got hit even harder than planned. By the time Clarence and I had worked our way to the front of the line, the harried serving committee had served well over 1,000. The staff looked shell-shocked.

What was worse in a town of Norwegians, they had run out of mashed potatoes.

Chapter 2

The Rise of a Prairie Town

Odd that potatoes ran short at the all-school reunion dinner in Halstad, for potatoes have played a big role in building the town. Not only have potatoes always been a daily staple on Halstad dinner tables, but the crop has contributed much to the Halstad economy over the past 100 years. So much, in fact, that youngsters in the middle of the century looked forward to up to two weeks of "potato vacation" per autumn, when school would be let out so that they could work in the fields picking potatoes and putting them in burlap sacks.

Potatoes were not only a part of Halstad's diet and economy. If you go back a ways, potatoes were one reason Halstad came into existence.

A bit of World History: When Columbus returned to Spain from the New World, he brought potatoes along home with him. The tuber was nutritious and easy to grow. It offered the peasantry of Europe a good-tasting, dietary improvement. The potato moved northward over the next two hundred years, finally reaching Norway in the mid-1700s.

Norwegians aren't known for their adventurous nature in dietary matters, but a crusading Lutheran clergyman named P. H. Hertzberg tirelessly promoted the potato in his sermons and in books as a solution to the nutritional deficits of Norwegian peasants. The food eventually caught on and became a staple.

The results were almost immediate. The vitamin C in potatoes made for healthier Norwegians. The live birth rate in Norway skyrocketed. Soon, there was no longer room on the rocky Norwegian farms for all of the offspring who reached adulthood.

The pressure of population built in the narrow fjords. Farms in Norway were too small in the first place. With the added population, if a farmer were to divide up his land among his offspring, the resulting tracts would be too small to support a family.

Stringent primogeniture laws were set up to keep farms intact. That meant that large numbers of young Norwegians, those who weren't the eldest son, had to find something else to do and somewhere else to live.

A natural outlet for the surplus potato-fed millions of northern Europe was the frontier of the United States. The Irish, also forced out of their country due to potato-related issues, came to the East Coast; but Germans,

Danes, Swedes, Finns, Norwegians and others flooded into the American Midwest.

Starting in Nebraska, Illinois, and Iowa, the northern European immigrants continually spread outward in search of new land. At the same time, the government was giving land to the railroads, who then sold it off cheaply to settlers. By 1871, waves of immigrants were attracted by this land to Northwestern Minnesota.

The ethnic groups stuck together. In Minnesota and North Dakota, you had German settlements, Swedish enclaves, and Norwegian towns, to name a few. When Halstad, Minnesota began to form in the early 1870s, it was Norwegian through and through.

Many of Halstad's Norwegian settlers had settled in Iowa and Illinois first, only to find the same problem there that caused them to move from Norway: There wasn't enough land to satisfy their hunger for wealth. So when the Red River Valley of the North opened up, and treeless, rich, virgin land became available for a reasonable price, many Norwegian immigrants uprooted a second time and moved north.

The settlers wrote back to Norway and appealed to their kin to come make their fortunes in the Red River Valley. Thus, Halstad caught some Norwegian immigrants on the first bounce and others on the second. Overall, more than 700,000 Norwegians immigrated to the American Upper Midwest from 1870-1930, a number which represented about forty percent of Norway's population at any one time during that period.

The Norwegians who came to Halstad soon found that Halstad's flood-enriched soil was ideal for growing their beloved potatoes. Although potatoes weren't always profitable as a cash crop, yielding what one farmer described as "five Ford years for every Cadillac year," they put good food on the table almost every year.

Halstad incorporated in 1883, only two years after the surrounding land was delineated by the Minnesota legislature as Norman County. The county's name arose because of the great number of Norwegian residents in the area. For many decades, no other county in Minnesota had a higher proportion of its folks born in Norway. The 2000 census showed that over fifty-seven percent of the county's residents were still of Norwegian descent over one hundred years after settlement.

Not long after 1883, names familiar to any 1952 Halstad area basketball fan start appearing in the Halstad township plat book. Serum. Hesby. Holm.

However, just because your name is Serum and you

live in Halstad doesn't mean that you are related to the other Serums down the road in Halstad. Surnames in the old country were often tied to farm location rather than ancestry. If you lived on the Serum farm when you left Norway, your name would be frozen as Serum at Ellis Island. If somebody moved onto the Serum farm in Norway after you left, they would get the Serum name, too. When the new family on the farm decided to emigrate thirty years later, their name might be recorded as Serum at Ellis Island as well.

The old Norwegian surname tradition explains why, in the little town of Halstad, there were two sets of Serums, a couple of families named Stennes, more than one bunch of Holms and two families of Uelands, all unrelated to the others bearing their name. The naming issue demonstrates something else: Not only was Halstad a Norwegian town, but most of its residents came from the same area of Norway. The immigrants tended to join their Old World neighbors when they got to the New World.

The hamlet of Halstad was lucky to have formed on the eventual route of the Great Northern rail line which ran parallel to the Red River. Dozens of hamlets had sprung up in Norman County during early settlement, and many were granted post offices, but most dried up quickly due to the lack of rail service. Meanwhile, towns on the rail line such as Halstad became centers of commerce for the surrounding farms.

There soon came to be plenty of farms. The grasslands of the Red River Valley were coveted due to the ability of the black gumbo soil to produce large crops of wheat. Even more important to settlers: Because there were no trees except for those growing on the slopes flanking the rivers, the land could be made ready for a crop immediately.

"One can plow for miles without touching a stone or a stump," according to one early farmer.

While people fifty miles to the east spent years—decades, in fact—grubbing stumps from their land so they could plant crops, the farmers in the Valley simply had to make sure their land was drained.

Although it was less troublesome than clearing stumps, drainage was no simple matter. Farmers who bought poorly drained land had to put in months and years of effort to dredge ditches to the nearest tributary of the Red River. The flatness of the land made farming easier, but the same flatness caused water, when it gathered, to move downstream at a deliberate pace.

The flatness was a shock to the new immigrants. Their home territory in Norway was exactly the opposite.

Norway has trees. And fjords. And the sea. And fresh flowing streams. The Red River Valley had none of the above. Compounding the sensory deprivation of living on the prairie were the long winters, as well as the requirement, which later continued as a tradition, that farm families live on the land they homesteaded and not in town. Thus, in a time before telephones, cars, and good roads, farm dwellers, especially women, were forced to spend the long winters isolated from human beings other than their immediate family.

The loneliness often became unbearable. Women on the farm might go weeks during winter in a tiny, windowless cabin listening to the howling wind—that is, if they were lucky enough to have a cabin. Often the first few winters of settlement were spent in a dugout—literally a cave—or in a sod hut. Warm as they were in winter, dirt-walled dwellings had to be about as dreary a way to spend five months of winter as you could imagine.

These were not the good old days. They were times of intense suffering, of questioning, of lonely people wondering what they had done. More than a few lost their sanity in the process. In addition, epidemics of typhoid, diphtheria, tuberculosis, and smallpox took many lives, particularly of children.

Adding to the despondency in the 1880s and 1890s, the winters were worse than usual. Grasshoppers completely destroyed several crops. Crops which did survive were difficult to get to market. And just when the crops did get to market, it seemed that the big boys in Minneapolis and Chicago conspired to lower the prices, sometimes to the point where the bill for shipping exceeded the revenue from the crop.

But from humble, harsh, and often horrendous beginnings on the prairie during the last two decades of the 19th century, a rudimentary civilization emerged. Once the settlers so much as got on their feet, they strove to build a society. Their first mission: Build churches.

Lutheran churches in Norman County, at first crude shacks strewn across the countryside, evolved by the late 1890s into beautiful gothic structures topped by enormous steeples. Inside the steeples were huge bells, custom-forged out east, brought in on trains, and raised into the steeples by precarious pulley systems. Most churches were soon equipped with pump organs, others with actual pipe organs. Some church buildings had stained glass. All had a beautiful painting of Jesus behind the altar.

Next on the settlers' agenda: Schools. Nothing better illustrates the progress of the small prairie town of

Halstad than the rapid improvement of school buildings. In the country, one-room, log schoolhouses gave way to frame buildings with bell towers by the mid-1890s. In the town of Halstad, a small schoolhouse was replaced by a large, two-story wood structure in 1884. This in turn was replaced by a truly imposing, beautifully designed, two-story brick schoolhouse in 1905. At the time it was built, it was Halstad's tallest structure. The brick building, surrounded by several additions, still stands today. It has been relegated to third place on the Halstad skyline, beneath the water tower and the grain elevator. Yet, it remains the most beautiful building in town.

Throughout the beginnings of the community, education seemed even more valued by Halstad's Norwegian settlers and their descendants than it was by those elsewhere in similar circumstances. For many years, Halstad was the smallest village in Minnesota to have an accredited high school.

Schools and churches wouldn't have been possible if farming didn't provide the people an adequate living. Indeed, the town of Halstad wouldn't have formed and grown if it weren't for the farms around it which supported its businesses, churches and school. By the 1890s, the plat book for Halstad township had taken shape. The land, originally in large, railroad-owned tracts, had been divided up into farms ranging in size from 160 to 400 acres. A few farmers held more than an entire section of 640 acres, but they were rare.

The American frontier, for all its hardships, had some of the highest live birth rates in the world at the time. As a result, the countryside, already peopled with farm families every 100 acres or so, would soon fill with their children. Good nutrition, lots of fresh air and relatively good sanitation helped keep people on the farms healthier than their city cousins of the day.

In the early 1900s, grains were the main cash crops, as they had been since settlement. Potatoes were on the rise, not just for the farm family's table but also as a cash crop. Every farm kept a few dairy cows, pigs, chickens, and sheep for the family's own use, and most all farmyards featured a large garden. Even when money was short, living on the farm meant a bountiful supply of good, fresh food.

Supported by the needs of farmers on the surrounding prairie, Halstad's Main Street businesses thrived in the early 1900s. Most anything you needed you could get in town, from fancy women's hats at the two millinery shops, to meals at the five cafes, to supplies at the several hardware stores.

As was the custom of the time, the furniture stores doubled as coffin suppliers. Helleloid Bros. Confectionary sold candy. By 1910, little Halstad had a bakery, a few meat markets, a liquor store, several saloons, a couple of drug stores, a dress shop, at least two banks, two barber shops, a printing office, a photography studio, a handful of auto and farm machinery dealers, and two hotels, as well as several general mercantiles and grocery stores.

Among the occupations present then which have since vanished: A blacksmith shop, a livery barn and several dray lines owned by men who hauled freight around town by carts, wagons, or by whatever means at their disposal.

Frequent fires and changes in ownership make establishing the exact number of businesses at any given time difficult. Many Halstad businesses, like a tin shop which sold "items made out of tin," didn't last long. But there is no doubt that Main Street Halstad was a busy place in the early 1900s. In addition to businesses, downtown featured an opera house, which, after it burned, was replaced by the Woodman Modern Theater, a Mason's lodge, a dance hall, a fire hall, and a temperance lodge.

As the 19th century turned into the 20th, Halstad's streets were mud and the sidewalks wooden, but the future was bright. Although Halstad never took on the boisterous mood of a boom-town—the Norwegian settlers were too stolid and worked too hard to survive to get that excited—the residents sent many letters to relatives in other parts of the United States and back in Norway: Come to Halstad to seek your fortune!

After 1900, Halstad civic organizations took off. A volunteer fire department. A men's chorus. A thirty-member community band. Hocus-pocus lodges such as the beard-growing "Brothers of the Brush" and the stylish "Sisters of the Swish." Sons of Norway, Daughters of Norway, Royal Neighbors of America.

The Norwegian Lutheran church was the main church in town, but the Methodist church on the west edge of town held Sunday evening services with lusty hymn singing which drew even the Lutheran youth.

Five decades in the future, town team baseball would be the biggest draw in town, but early in the century, the area was full enough with people to support township baseball. Instead of one team for the entire town of Halstad, there were about a half-a-dozen teams spread around the countryside, and they played each other, sometimes on pastures or on fallow fields which were harrowed into dusty submission for the purpose of playing ball.

Any excuse to get together would suffice. The men came to Ladies Aid meetings. Temperance groups held alcohol-free dances. Luther Leagues drew big crowds. Traveling orators could fill the theater. And because of Halstad's fortunate position on a prominent Great Northern Line, the opera house was sometimes able to book big musical or theater acts which were passing through from Minneapolis to Winnipeg.

There was a sense in the small prairie towns in the early 1900s that you were part of something growing, something big, something new. The incredible civic energy with which small town residents built their beautiful churches, heavily ornamented city halls, and stately brick schools came, in part, from their well-honed work ethic, but also from a sense that they were part of the next big thing.

On the farm, families worked together to provide themselves lots of good food and a minimal living, an arrangement which today seems quaint, almost Amish. Assuming that Dad didn't drink to excess (an even more common problem at the time than it is today), or that Mom wasn't suicidally depressed (also a common problem at the time, though one which was hushed up), farm life was full of both hard work and good fun.

What entertainment was there? Other people and only other people. You had to get together with others to have fun. Homes were open to neighbor kids and neighbor adults, all of whom dropped in freely and fully expected to be fed a meal appropriate for the time of day. Communication was blissfully slow between farms. If you decided to stay overnight with your school friend, you stayed overnight and nobody at home worried that you didn't call.

In accordance with Thomas Jefferson's Northwest Ordinances, newly surveyed land was laid out in mile-by-mile squares. In the Red River Valley, no natural features exist to prevent those squares from being perfectly uniform. In fact, those who've grown up in the Red River Valley come to think that God intended the world to be laid out in perfect mile-by-mile squares. Anything else is confusing.

By the early 1900s, the roads had been built around each square and the farms were close enough together that it became a tradition on Sunday evenings for young farm people to walk around the entire four-mile section, singing Stephen Foster songs as they went, picking up walkers as they passed by their farm and dropping them off at home again the next time around.

Country schools were a center of community life. Around Halstad, at least nine country schools operated in the area which eventually became the Halstad school district. There was the Wilson school, the Aalgaard school, the Serum school, the Bluebird school, the Hellerud school, the Foss school, and the Hoiland school. The nicknames were informal and could change with time. For formal matters such as meeting notices and correspondence with state officials, each district had a number. The one-room schoolhouses were used at various times for church, club meetings, plays and ice cream socials, even dances.

Although the old country school is the subject of much romance and sentiment having to do with breaking the ice in the water pail during winter and dipping pony-tails in inkwells, the quality of the instruction was pretty spotty. Teachers were trained for no more than a few months. Often, teachers were barely eighteen years old, younger than some of their pupils. If you had a kind and competent teacher, things could be wonderful. Students would put on plays and sing and have fun at recess and learn their multiplication tables all at once. But if you had a sour teacher with a chip on his or her shoulder and a quick willow switch, an entire generation of kids in a neighborhood might go sour as well.

If you didn't mind the cold walks to school during

the middle of winter, being a kid on a prairie farm had to have been fun. Instead of the doting, over-protective, over-involved parents so prevalent today, kids on the farm back then were pretty much ignored—at least until they could help with the chores and become of economic value. There were advantages to being ignored, as any builder of tree houses can attest, but there were disadvantages as well.

Safety of children was of little concern, at least compared to today. Death was a constant among children, and, although the grief was real when a child died of illness or in an accident, it didn't translate into general worry.

"We were a dime a dozen," said one Norman County resident of life as a child in the early 1900s, "and we knew it."

Deprivations? There were still many, but they were shared equally by all: Outdoor toilets at thirty below zero, severe childhood infections which went untreated by penicillin, intractable teeth problems, inadequate eye glasses. There were social problems, and little in the way of formal recourse. Abused women, who were considered property and whose word didn't hold water in court, or abused children, who again, were considered the father's property to do with as he pleased, stood little chance of escaping their situation. As idyllic as it might have been to have lived in Halstad in 1900, you wouldn't have wanted to be born there, or anywhere at the time, with any sort of major disability, medical problem, or family dysfunction.

By the early 1900s, Halstad's population had reached the number around which it would hover for a century: 595. Looking at population figures of the town itself for the past one hundred years, one might get the impression that the number of people has stayed constant. However, in the surrounding countryside the story is different.

By 1915, the countryside surrounding Halstad was as full of people as it was ever going to be. The membership rolls at East Marsh River Church seven miles east of town reached their all-time peak in about 1915. Enrollment at the many country schools reached its apex at the same time. The flat, treeless prairie was dotted with farm places every quarter- to half-a-mile. The county's population, depending upon which newspaper you read, showed that Norman County had as many as 15,000 residents.

And that was too many. The number wasn't sustainable. To keep that many people busy in Norman County, the farms would have had to stay small. Farm machinery would have had to stay primitive, and prices for commodities would have had to stay relatively high.

None of the above happened. Farms were forced to become more efficient and much larger. Machinery increased relentlessly in size and speed. And farm prices over the years slid, in real terms, steadily down. So, as technology improved, the countryside was doomed to be slowly drained of its people and a good share of the vitality it enjoyed in 1915.

If it weren't for dramatic larger world events, the decline of the small town from 1915 forward might have been gradual, gentle, and barely perceptible. As it turned out, the road downhill was bumpy and at times steep.

Chapter 3

Tough Times

When the Great War broke out in Europe in August of 1914, its effect in Halstad, Minnesota, was to usher in the most prosperous years ever seen. With Europe's agriculture torn up by war, the price of wheat rose to 98 cents per bushel, a level unheard of at the time. For the first three years of the war in Europe, the United States stayed on the sidelines. Prosperity on the farm came without any apparent price.

In 1917, Congress declared war. President Wilson led the United States into the gigantic conflict across the Atlantic. Bands played on the train platform of nearly every small farm town as boys were sent off to the barracks. For farm towns, the loss of boys wasn't as bad as it would be during the next world-wide conflagration twenty-four years later. Farm production was seen as so important to the war effort that the Army handed out farm-related draft deferments quite liberally. Unlike World War II, World War I took disproportionately fewer boys off the farm that it took from the city. So, at the onset of American involvement in World War I, before the casualty lists began to roll in, it was possible to think that good times were still on. Farm prices, already at record levels, rose even higher when President Wilson guaranteed American farmers a $2 per bushel price for their wheat.

As was Wilson's intention, American farmers immediately devoted most of their acres to wheat. Many farmers quietly became wealthy and began to improve their property. During the era of 1914-1918 some of the largest, grandest, square farmhouses in the Red River Valley were built, including many in and around Halstad, as well as a raft of graineries, chicken coops, and other capital improvements. Once mere gatherings of tiny shacks, Norman County farmyards became showplaces.

During the years of 1914-1918, farmers in Minnesota were more likely to own cars and have telephones than people in the city of Minneapolis. Farmers had money. The prosperity spread to Main Street of the small town, for farming was the entire basis of the economy in Norman County and in the town of Halstad. As farming went, so went the town. In the years just before 1918, save for the worry of having many local boys off at war, there was prosperity like there never had been before.

The long-term prospects for small farmers were dim, but few in 1918 knew it. What farmers found out in a hurry was that the short-term prospects were no good, either.

After World War I, price supports were lowered. By 1920, the supports disappeared altogether. With Europe again producing wheat, surpluses quickly mounted. The price of wheat crashed.

Suddenly wheat, so profitable during the war that many farmers planted it exclusively, cost more to raise than it brought in at harvest. Farm land values plummeted. Farmers who borrowed to buy land found that they owed far more than the land was worth. As a result, in farm country, many banks failed in the decade before the crash of 1929.

Small town newspaper editors in the 1920s understood the gravity of the problem. The entire foundation of the small communities, towns which had been so prosperous, so progressive, so on-the-move only years before, was threatened. As the back pages of the local paper filled with foreclosure notices, the front page trumpeted potential savior crops: Flax, alfalfa, grasses, sugar beets, potatoes. Although most farms had a few dairy cows to provide the family milk, reports came in of large dairy operations in other parts of Minnesota which were raking in large profits. "Build your herd," cried the papers. "Our survival as a town depends upon it."

Whenever a financial shakedown comes to farm country, the first foreclosures often weed out the greedy speculators and sloppy businessmen, the type of people whose neighbors might think had it coming. But as the 1920s wore on, low commodity prices didn't just cull out the fly-by-night operators. The downswing got the solid people, too. In the end, some townships in Norman County had fewer than a half-dozen farms remaining under the same ownership for the duration of the decade.

So, while the rest of the country was preoccupied by the Roaring '20s, the Charleston, *The Great Gatsby*, Charles Lindberg, and Babe Ruth, Norman County and other grain-farming regions entered tough times which went unnoticed by the world at large. After the prosperity on the farm before 1920, losing so much ground in such a short time to the suddenly-thriving cities was a bitter pill to swallow.

In addition to the rapidly declining farm economy, the influenza epidemic of 1918, which killed more people worldwide than did World War I, hit Norman County hard, wiping out several families in their entirety. The fresh air in the countryside provided no apparent protection from the plague, and now we know why: The virus was transmitted by birds.

Many of the soldiers who went off to war, having seen the world, and seeing, accurately, that the farm was not a place to prosper, never returned. As a result of the flu and the loss of the soldiers, after 1920 the population of rural Minnesota saw its first decline after fifty years of rapid growth. The decline would continue with few pauses for the next eighty-five years.

The trend was national. The year 1920 was also when city population first exceeded farm population in the United States. At that point, the division of people between farm and city was half and half. As of 2007, less than 1% of the American populace lives on an active farm.

The economics changed in the small town, and so did the psychology. Sinclair Lewis' novel *Main Street*, published in the 1920s, went a long ways towards puncturing the somewhat overinflated balloon of small-town farm culture. By lampooning the small-mindedness of the small Minnesota farm town of Gopher Prairie, modeled on his hometown of Sauk Center, Minnesota, Lewis took on what was at the time a formidable target. A modern reader unfamiliar with the prosperity and cultural power of small towns in the era from 1900-1920 might wonder why Lewis didn't save his bombast for something bigger. But at the time, Lewis voiced the rebellious discontent of roughly half the nation's youth, for the small town was where over half the nation's youth had grown up.

The stock market crash of 1929 hit. The immediate effect in the Red River Valley: Potato prices collapsed. After the crash, as if on cue, the rains stopped for the better part of ten years. For the beleaguered farmers of Norman County it was just more of the same—plus drought. Farms continued to change hands, although Depression-weary bankers eventually became a little more tolerant than they were in the 1920s. They didn't want to own the worthless land, either. Better to string the farmers along and hope for a better year next year.

Even when there was a crop, however paltry, there was no price. One Norman County farmer remembers getting paid 2 cents per bushel of potatoes. Another remembers his father selling a train car full of sheep—and instead of receiving a check, he got a bill for the shipping. The low point was the hot, dry summer of 1936, which broke all records for days over 100 degrees in the Halstad area—as well as the following winter, which broke all records for bone-chilling cold.

Grim times on the prairie. But then President Franklin Roosevelt introduced programs to help farmers. Struggling small communities also benefited from Works

Progress Administration projects. Using WPA funds and workers, Halstad added a gymnasium and classrooms to its school in 1939. When the roof sprang a leak a few years later, it was blamed on those sub-par WPA workers. Even so, everybody was glad to have a new gym.

Just as the stock market crash of 1929 seemed to set off a world-wide drought, the outbreak of World War II in Europe coincided with the return of the rains. Although good old-fashioned gully-washers didn't return until the summer of 1940, a year when some crops were actually washed out, a few farmers in the Halstad area had good enough crops in 1938 to pay off their entire farms in one fell swoop.

And then, Pearl Harbor. In World War I, farm deferments kept many farm boys home while the city boys were drafted in greater numbers. But after the onset of World War II, farm deferments were less frequent. Over 100 people served from Halstad alone. Crops were good during the war, but farmers had a tough time finding enough labor to bring in the harvest. The rains returned with the war, but to describe the World War II years as good times on the farm, even if you didn't have a son—or four—fighting overseas, was to ignore reality.

Take tires. Rubber was rationed. Tires were scarce.

To get your grain to town, you needed a truck with tires. But say on the way to town you blow out a tire, a misfortune which was more likely than not to occur. Early in the war, you might have been able to borrow a tire from a neighbor to get your truck to town. By 1944, however, no neighbor in his right mind would let his neighbor borrow a tire for any reason whatsoever. There are tales of trucks sitting at the side of the road, full of grain, for the entire winter, unable to make the final leg of the trip to the grain elevator due to a flat tire.

Sugar was rationed during the war, even though there was no actual shortage and nobody has ever figured out why rationing was needed. Housewives had to try to preserve fruits from their "Victory Gardens" with limited sugar. In one case across the river from Halstad in North Dakota, a woman was denied sugar because the rationing board had a dim view of her canning abilities.

Gas was rationed. If you didn't get enough to get your crops off, you had to go through the local rationing board to get more. If they didn't like how you farmed, you might have to fight for your allotment.

Rationing boards weren't always fair. You can imagine putting a committee of locals in charge of which neighbor gets gas and which neighbor gets sugar. However, complaining about injustices in sugar rations when the boys were overseas giving their lives wasn't seemly. There was an appeals process, but it was cumbersome and seldom used.

Yes, the rains returned during war. Yes, prices for farm commodities were well-supported at profitable levels. And yes, the struggles on the farm due to rationing and lack of labor paled in comparison to the troubles faced by the boys on the battlefield. Even so, life on the farm during World War II could only be described as an exercise in frustration, and often deprivation.

Old Christ Sulerud of Halstad rode the roller coaster all the way to the top and back down again. An orphan in Norway, Sulerud made his way to Ada, Minnesota, at age sixteen. He worked at the hardware store and attended English classes at night. After his brother John joined him, the pair formed a partnership and moved to Halstad where they purchased a hardware store. At that time, Christ Sulerud also started a dairy farm which became well-known as one of the best in the area. Sulerud Hardware became one of the best-stocked stores in Norman County. And Christ Sulerud was elected to the Minnesota Legislature on the Prohibition ticket in 1908 and 1910.

In 1913, Sulerud built the biggest house in town, which still stands. His wife Emma bore five children. Sulerud was community-minded, helping to organize the building of the grain elevator, the creamery, the high school, and a bridge across the Red River.

Christ and Emma Sulerud insisted that their children be educated. Their eldest daughter Hazel taught high school English. Their second daughter Gladys taught music. Son Clark earned a degree in business at the University of Minnesota, then added a law degree at the University of North Dakota and went to work for various banks. Son George became a professor of agriculture at Oregon State University. Son Lester worked on the farm.

The Suleruds were a success. Then came 1929. Christ Sulerud had put every possible acre of his land into potatoes. After the stock market crash in October, the potato market collapsed. The Suleruds were in danger of losing everything, including Sulerud Hardware.

In desperation, Christ Sulerud called his three sons home to help with the family businesses. All three moved back to Halstad, giving up their chosen careers. They worked for a meager salary from the family corporation. They settled down and started families.

With the help of his sons, Christ Sulerud managed to hang onto the family's farm land and the hardware store. But before they had a chance to turn things around, Christ Sulerud was stricken with cancer. He died in 1936, when the Great Depression hit its depths.

By coming home, the Sulerud boys had taken a risk. They had already become successes on their own, but the allure of succeeding on their home turf drew them back. Although they never expressed regrets, and the Suleruds were a big part of the Halstad community for the rest of their days, they never made it big. The hardware store was not able to provide an ample living for three families, and only one of the brothers had any interest in farming. As a result, much of the Sulerud land was sold off for $40 per acre, rich land which quickly multiplied in value once good times returned.

Perhaps the Sulerud boys figured they could do as well as their father. But when Halstad had three hardware stores in 1952, more than it needed, with one of them the means of support for three Sulerud families, you have to wonder if Clark, George, and John wondered late at night about their decision to give up promising careers and cast their lot with a small farming town on the prairie.

Chapter 4

A Gem of a Time

Fast forward to 1951. World War II was over. The Korean Conflict, which claimed 52,000 American lives in just more than two years, was dragging on, but because it was fought in the shadow of the larger world war which had ended six years previously, the war in Korea simply didn't loom large enough to interfere with the sense that good times were back.

On the farms around Halstad, good times were indeed back. After twenty-five years of varied and constant trials and tribulations, labor was plentiful, prices were stable, rains were regular, and, after the government lifted war restrictions, farmers were finally able to use their profits to mechanize. Pull-type combines run by one man replaced threshing machines run by a crew of twenty. The time it took to plow a field was slashed by the use of larger, stronger tractors. Improvements in machinery meant that a 300-acre farm could be managed easily by a family of average size and ambition.

The arrival of electricity was also a boon to farm families. Although the city of Halstad was served by a power plant from the 1920s, the Rural Electric Administration (REA) brought power into Halstad's rural areas beginning in 1941. Rural electrification paused during the war, but it was finished up soon thereafter. Electrification probably represents the biggest single improvement ever made in farm life. Electricity improved the life of farmwives in previously unimagined ways: Refrigeration. Electric ranges. Electric washers. Electric lights. Once the war ended and appliances became broadly available, the sales of appliances to farm houses from the local dealers became a thriving part of the town's economy.

Farmers with dairy cows now had the option of using electric milking machines instead of milking by hand. Power tools, which some old-timers resisted, slashed the time it took to build a shed, a chicken coop, or a new house. The terrific hard work on the farm, which had been compounded by the overwhelming difficulties of the Great Depression, was relieved as much by technological advance as it was by the return of the rains, the end of the war, and generally good prices.

Halstad's economic situation was helped by a series of good potato years. Potato warehouses, set deep in the ground to keep them cool, sprang up near the railroad tracks in town, next to the livestock pens where farmers had long brought in cattle, pigs, and sheep for shipment.

In addition to potatoes, a new crop gained popularity in the Red River Valley: sugar beets. And one of the first generation of sugar beet farmers was Martin Akason of Halstad.

Throughout the Depression, Martin Akason was the Husky Oil dealer in Halstad. He, his wife, and their two boys, Jimmy and Bill, lived on the edge of town in a small, rented house owned by a bachelor who lived upstairs. Martin Akason struggled through the lean years like everybody else, but when the war came and farming improved, he saw opportunity.

Martin Akason became a "sidewalk farmer." That is, he lived in Halstad but rented land on the North Dakota side of the river which he farmed. It was a struggle to get started from scratch, of course. He had to purchase machinery and learn the trade on the run. But Martin Akason was a determined and able man with a personality as big as his formidable frame.

Martin Akason's oldest son Jimmy was great help. Jimmy grew up in a hurry: From the time he was eight years old, he spent long hours alone on the tractor, tilling fields in North Dakota, miles away from the little house on the edge of Halstad.

Although some Red River Valley farmers had tried

sugar beets earlier in the century, the crop hadn't taken hold. But with the climate and the soils in the Valley ideal for beets, it was a matter of time before a sugar industry developed and factories were built to process the beets into white sugar. Red River Valley sugar beets eventually would grow into a billion-dollar industry. Today, the Valley supplies fifteen percent of the sugar consumed in the United States.

In the early 1950s, however, the Valley's sugar beet industry was still in its infancy. Harvest equipment was primitive. The long rows of beets had to be hand weeded all summer. Once harvest arrived and they were plowed out of the ground, one row at a time, the tops had to be sliced off by hand. Finally, the big beets, which can weigh up to ten pounds each, had to be hauled away in carts.

For this back-breaking labor, most of the beet farmers, including Martin Akason, hired migrant workers from Texas. The migrants arrived packed in canvas-covered trucks. Some farmers simply cleaned out a chicken coop to house the migrants, but Esther Akason insisted that the twenty Mexicans the Akasons hired be housed in decent, clean cabins.

From an early age, young Jimmy Akason remembers the migrants calling him "Meester Yeem." The Mexicans knew to treat the boss's son with respect, and young Jimmy enjoyed the rapport. After hoeing the beets during the early summer, the migrants went to Michigan to pick cherries, then on to Wisconsin to pick pickles, only to return to Halstad for the beet harvest in late September before returning to Texas for the winter.

Work on farms around Halstad was still hard in the 1950s, and money was, by present day standards, pretty scarce. But wealth is relative. Compared to the previous twenty-five years, life on the farm was overwhelmingly good. And, for the first time since 1918, conditions on the farm seemed to be getting more prosperous all the time. Good times on the farm meant good times in Halstad.

Halstad's citizens supported a raft of community improvement projects with very little opposition. The church benefited first. By the end of the Depression, the Methodist Church had folded and Lutheranism was the only religion in town. Between the three congregations, Halstad Lutheran in town, and Augustana and East Marsh River in the countryside, the parish had 1,200 members. Together, the parish churches ponied up for a new parsonage for their parish pastor, Rev. Carl Opsahl, in 1949. It was built without the use of power tools, by a silent, meticulous Norwegian carpenter from Halstad named Orlando Serum.

When it was decided that Pastor Opsahl needed a better car, it was no problem to raise the funds. One Sunday morning, the proud church president presented a surprised Rev. Opsahl with the keys to a black, four-door, 1951 Ford.

Charity auctions for various causes raised surprising amounts of money in the early 1950s. At one such event, a package of lefse was bid up to $6. Essentially a tortilla made out of potatoes, lefse is a bland Norwegian delicacy, the charms of which can easily escape those without Norse blood. That one package would go for an inflation-adjusted $60 is more a tribute to the extravagance of the bidders than the desirability of the product.

The school was next to be improved. The Halstad school population, swollen by students coming in from the countryside, quickly outgrew the 1939 WPA addition. From 1940 to 1951, twelve country schools had closed, sending their students into the Halstad school. The elementary school population rose from 97 to 150 during the decade.

More students from the countryside began to attend high school. For high school, one had to go to town. Following the opening of Halstad High School in 1906, students from the countryside who desired a high school education, most of them female, would board at homes in town for the winter. After World War II, as high school became more popular for both genders, buses were sent out in the countryside to pick up students from first through twelfth grades. Although at least one country school district maintained a one-room school for its elementary students into the 1960s, most one-room country schools in what became Halstad Consolidated School District No. 18 were closed by 1951.

With the added students in the brick schoolhouse, space was tight. Public meetings were held to address the problem. With no significant opposition, a bond issue for a large new addition was proposed. It passed by a vote of 133-17 in March of 1951, and new classrooms were ready for use midway through the next school year.

Halstad residents had money to remodel their homes. In 1951, the Valley Journal reported dozens of improvements, and said "the trend in house painting is moving away from the traditional white." The Bernhagens painted their house red. The Paulsruds went from white to yellow, and the Breilands went with green. Several homes replaced their foundations. Others added porches and sun parlors, and four families on "the other side of the tracks" added shiny new asbestos siding.

"We didn't know any different," says retired teacher Darrel Hesby, sitting in his Wayzata, Minnesota, living room with his wife Janet, reflecting upon his years growing up in Halstad. The Hesbys' current home sits near the old downtown of the now ritzy suburb of Wayzata, a few hundred yards from Lake Minnetonka. Newly-built townhomes one block away sell for $2 million. Given the circumstances of his youth, Hesby seems amazed by his present surroundings.

Darrel Hesby was raised in a modest house jammed against the sidewalk on one of downtown Halstad's side streets. In the early part of the century, the building had housed a doctor's office as well as his living quarters. In the 1940s and early 1950s, it was home to Grandma Hesby's boarding house. The building, now empty, stands to the present day.

Grandma Hesby's boarding house was a center of activity in Halstad in the early 1950s. Mrs. Hesby cooked for her retired husband, her son, Allen, his wife Joyce, and son Darrel, as well as her daughter, all of whom lived under the same roof. She also served many of the single men of the town two meals a day. Grandma Hesby's wasn't an official restaurant with a sign out front, but the men about town knew where they could get a grand, home-cooked meal for a quarter.

When the 1939 addition was built on the school, the WPA boys working on the project would jump on their motorcycles at noon and roar across the tracks to Grandma Hesby's for a full meal of meat, mashed potatoes, veggies, and a dessert of apple pie. The scene was repeated at quitting time a few hours later. Unemployed bachelors would sit in chairs outside Grandma Hesby's front door and play cards and smoke cigarettes.

Grandma Hesby also catered, although the practice wasn't known by the term at the time. In most towns, the local Ladies Aid cooked their own meals for their gatherings. In Halstad, the Ladies Aid meetings were catered by Grandma Hesby. For such affairs, she would produce potato salad by the vat—at the same time she was preparing a noon meal for her family and the men of the town.

At threshing time, it was tradition for the host farm to produce a tremendous meal for the crew of men. Around Halstad, however, many farmwives responsible for feeding threshing crews simply picked up the food ready-made from Grandma Hesby.

Grandma Hesby's output was prodigious. She was in the kitchen from dawn to dusk. And she did all of her business out of a single coin purse. After he was old enough to figure out what was going on, young Darrel asked Grandma Hesby if they made enough money to survive. "Oh, we get along," she said cheerfully, and that was that.

Hard work was all Grandma Hesby had ever known. Her schooling ended with the eighth grade in Norway. She crossed the ocean and ended up in Halstad at age fifteen. She never attended school again.

"You look back now," Darrel says, "and think the whole arrangement was a little odd." At the time, it was what Darrel knew, and it seemed workable enough.

Wealth is relative. To young Darrel Hesby, life was full of good things. Grandma Hesby's good food. The company of dozens of interesting people at the dining room table each day. Complete freedom to roam the town of Halstad as he pleased, playing baseball and basketball, fishing in the river, and generally raising Cain.

"There was a simplicity about the time," Hesby says today, echoing the comments of many of his fellow Starting Five.

Darrel's best friend, Jimmy Akason, lived just down the street. From the earliest years, Jimmy and Darrel would take cookie boxes, fold the flap over the living room door of Grandma Hesby's house, and use the box as a basket for raucous games of indoor basketball.

"We almost wrecked that house," says Jim Akason today.

Eventually, Martin Akason set up a basket in front of his house for Jimmy and his friends. The basket was only eight feet tall. The reduced height allowed young Jimmy and Darrel to dunk the basketball from an early age.

Darrel Hesby and Jimmy Akason were town kids. Those who've grown up in a small town know there's a big difference between town kids and country kids. To be a town kid meant you grew up earlier and were more world-wise than country kids. No matter how upright your household, town kids roamed the streets freely and were exposed early to people who swore, smoked, drank, and gambled. They hovered around any new and novel arrivals from out of town. As a result of their cosmopolitan surroundings, town kids developed confidence at an earlier age than their country counterparts. Some town kids were downright brash.

Parents allowed their kids to roam free around Halstad because they knew that anything untoward would be reported to them within minutes. There wasn't a house in town that was locked. A kid who felt threatened or who had bumped his head or skinned her knee could run inside the nearest house and be tended to as if that house were home.

Country kids, on the other hand, grew up isolated from all but their nearest neighbors. They went to school in the one-room schoolhouse for up to eight years with a handful of those same neighbor kids. Seldom did they have a chance to mingle with strangers.

When the summer came, country kids played with whomever was there. In town there were kids everywhere. In the country, if the neighbors didn't have children your age, you were stuck with siblings. You might get to town with the rest of the family on Saturday night, but in all likelihood you spent most of the rest of the week on the farm helping Dad or in the kitchen helping Mom.

As the one-room schoolhouses closed, one by one, and the country kids came to school in town, there was more than a little sectarian strife. Country kids were usually a bit shy. Town kids sometimes interpreted the shyness as stupidity, and it took time for the country kids to come out of their shell and throw their weight around a bit. You had to in order to survive in the dog-eat-dog, town-school environment. And the town kids eventually learned that the country kids, quiet as they were, had long, simmering memories for sly comments like "dumb country kid!" An elbow to the ribs in basketball practice in ninth grade might be a long-deferred payback for a sneer about "you dumb farm kid" on the playground in fifth grade.

But whether you were a town kid or a country kid, the early fifties, to use the words of Carol Henderson Serum, wife of Halstad basketball player and baseball catcher Dale Serum, was a "gem of a time to grow up" in and around a town such as Halstad. Although the population of the town and its surrounding farms peaked in 1915, the beauty of the town was at its peak in the 1950s. The barren Old West prairie village was now forested by majestic, mature, American Elm whose arches turned Halstad's narrow streets into shaded cathedrals. The attractive, old, downtown buildings were nearly all in use, as were the towering grain elevators and the half-buried potato warehouses along the tracks.

In addition to Grandma Hesby's boarding house, there were five cafes. The three hardware stores in Halstad were complemented by a handful of auto dealers, bars, mercantile stores, and as many as four grocery stores. Dress shops, shoe shops, and a jewelry store came and went during the era as well.

Dozens of veterans recently back from World War II added to the town's vigor. Returned veteran Larry Foley used a government loan from the GI bill to start a new hardware store, giving Halstad three hardware stores for the first time since 1920. Other veterans worked at local businesses under training programs subsidized by the government. One was paid twenty dollars per week by the government to work at the Halstad drug store. Another worked at the seed house. Overall, the veterans had a little money in their pockets and plenty of time to have fun.

After a period of near dormancy during World War II, the membership of the American Legion Post in Halstad expanded to 99 active members in the late 1940s. The vets didn't just hold meetings to say "aye" to the Treasurer's report, either. Eager to spice up life in the old home town, they put up a big tent on a vacant lot on the south edge of town in 1947 and sponsored dances every summer Saturday night. The wood floor, purchased from a defunct roller rink in neighboring Perley, was also good for roller skating, which was held other nights of the week.

The temporary tent was a hassle, and the veterans dreamed of a permanent "clubroom and recreation center." In 1949, construction started on a 50' x 120' Quonset structure built entirely with volunteer labor. The vets used their pull to get free gravel from the county gravel pit. They scored used lights from a department store in Fargo. The rafters were purchased for a discount.

In the end, the Legion Recreation Center was heated by two "automated oil furnaces," an exhaust system which could change the air in the building every fifteen minutes, a "fully equipped modern kitchen," and what was described as the finest sound system around.

Knotty pine lined the walls to an eight-foot height, and above that were bare rafters. Although plans were to put in a false ceiling, when Duke Ellington played the joint, he told the manager, "Don't you mess with that ceiling." He considered the acoustics in the LRC to be about perfect.

Duke Ellington wasn't the only big name to play the LRC. Rex Allen stopped by one evening for an impromptu concert. The Dorsey Brothers, the Glenn Miller Band, and other national acts supplemented the dozens of local dance orchestras which thrilled the overflow crowds at the LRC.

Legion member Bardulf Ueland was hired to manage the building on a temporary basis. He did so well that whenever he submitted his resignation, which seemed to be every two months, it was refused. Ueland had a knack for publicity and for finding good acts. One dance, at which Whoopee John's Orchestra played, sold over 800 tickets.

The *Norman County Index*, the newspaper of record in the county seat of Ada, anointed the efforts of the veterans by editorializing: "Their building became a reality because of an organized effort by a group of men who had fulfilled their obligations of protecting the welfare and safety of the nation and who are continuing to carry out their obligations to the community in which they live."

The veterans were assisted by dozens of community members. "I wheeled in a lot of concrete to that place," says Halstad resident Wally Oien, who was a teenager at the time.

The LRC dances pulled people from a wide area. In 1952, they took a poll: One Saturday night dance in Halstad drew partiers from 31 area towns.

Not everybody was on board the LRC bandwagon. The LRC dances were controversial. Although booze wasn't sold at the LRC, it was present in sometimes plentiful amounts. There was a general air of debauchery, both in the hall and out in the parking lot. Young people smoked. And the young men got drunk and fought. You didn't show up there if you wanted to play high school sports. You didn't show up there if you wanted to maintain a spotless reputation. And you didn't show up there if you wanted to be confirmed in the Lutheran faith by Rev. Carl Opsahl.

To be fair to Rev. Opsahl, he was just doing his job. And the job of a small-town Lutheran minister in the early 1950s was to be a guardian of the town's morality. Even if the Lutheran seminaries were moving steadily to the left, Lutheran pastors in the small towns knew they were expected to represent upright living to all and speak out against sin whenever and wherever it reared its ugly head.

Rev. Opsahl took his role seriously. He never left the house without a tie. He maintained a serious demeanor. And he weighed in on the great issues of the day. When the liquor question came to a vote in 1951, Rev. Opsahl wrote letters to the editor and held meetings in favor of making Halstad a dry town. Protected by secret ballot, the voters, many of whom filled the pews of Rev. Opsahl's Halstad Lutheran on Sunday, rejected the measure by a wide margin. Liquor would stay, but most of the parishioners, no matter how they voted, would likely have been disappointed if Rev. Opsahl hadn't opposed it. It was the preacher's job to oppose liquor, card playing, smoking, dancing, movies, and all other forms of morally questionable behavior, no matter how much his flock loved to engage in all of the above.

When on a beautiful summer evening, a neighbor girl brought out a bunch of sheet music of Broadway show tunes, and young Paul Opsahl brought out his trumpet from the parsonage, and other neighbor kids brought out their band instruments and started tooting away, it wasn't long before Rev. Opsahl appeared in his suit and tie to put an end to the debauchery—not because the kids were making too much noise, but because they were not to indulge in that sort of music.

And yet, the town loved Carl Opsahl unreservedly. Despite his insistence upon a set of rules, it was apparent to all that he cared deeply about his job, and in particular, that he cared deeply about the town's young. His sermons weren't hellfire and brimstone, but they were interesting enough to increase church attendance and participation in church activities.

As so often happens with a successful small-town minister, Carl had a wife who brimmed with charisma. His sternness was softened a great deal by his warm-hearted wife, Olina. Mrs. Opsahl's charm made her an immediate community leader.

"She talked to you like you were the only person in the world," said one woman who grew up in Halstad, herself not a churchgoing type.

Together, the Opsahls ministered to a parish of 1,200. Most memorably for those of school age at the time, the couple hosted Luther League gatherings for the town's youth which filled the new parsonage to overflowing. Almost everybody showed up. The memories the kids have of those times and the Opsahls are uniformly positive.

"Mrs. Opsahl emphasized excellence," according to Janet Sulerud Hesby, who graduated from Halstad High in 1952. "They both instilled in you that you could do big things."

The Opsahls brought energy to the town and showed interest in the town's youth. At a time when many of the old Norwegian parents didn't spend a lot of time "relating" to their children, Carl and Olina Opsahl's devotion to the kids brought them not just respect, but a great deal of appreciation from those children long after they grew up.

Even droll catcher Dale Serum, who had no time for Carl Opsahl's strictures on movies and card playing, appreciated Carl's concern, for when Opsahl left his job as Army chaplain after the war he managed to bring with him to Halstad about a dozen high-quality leather baseball gloves. Included was a real catcher's mitt, a boon to young Serum, who for some time before had to make do with a mitt his father Orlando had sewn out of a horse blanket and used overalls. "We were glad to see them come to town," Serum said with a wry smile.

The best of Halstad was on display during everybody's favorite time of the week: Saturday night. Going to town on Saturday nights in the early 1950s was a much-awaited event for people of all ages.

After finishing the chores and taking their weekly bath, farm families jumped in the car and roared across the gravel roads to town. Competition was keen for a parking space on Main Street where the people-watching was the best. By later in the evening, the streets in the residential areas were lined with cars as well, and it was tough to find a parking spot in the entire town.

What was the excuse for the Saturday night splurge, an important weekly ritual in every small farm town in the Upper Midwest at the time? One theory is that many farmwives of the time didn't drive. Saturday night, when Dad was free, was their night to come to town and stock up on groceries. Meanwhile, Dad might stop in at the saloon for a beer, or three, and the kids would run amok, using the nickels Dad gave them to get into such harmless mischief as throwing water balloons at passing cars.

The movie theater would fill for a double feature. Stores stayed open late into the evenings. Drawings were held just before closing as a way of keeping the people in town longer so they might shop more. Some Halstad Saturday night promotions in the 1950s wouldn't pass muster today: Community Club members brought a bag of live chickens up to the roof of the bank and tossed them one-by-one to the crowd below. If you caught one, it was yours to butcher.

"Worthless leghorns," complains long-time Halstad resident Roger Stole, fifty-five years later. Stole remembers catching a chicken only to have it snatched away from him by a woman with five kids whose husband had left her. "I didn't object," he said, "she needed it more than I did."

Wally Oien remembers a Saturday night battle with a greased pig, another promotion. "They poured used graphite oil over the thing and turned her loose," Oien recalls. He caught the pig on Erwin Warner's lawn, only to have difficulty wrestling the animal back to contest headquarters. By the end of the night, Oien was so greased up that "you couldn't tell in the picture which was me and which was the pig."

Later Saturday evening, a dance would crank up at the Legion Recreation Center. Good Lutherans avoided the LRC dances, but more lax Lutherans and out-oftowners, both of whom were plentiful, danced late into the night to local dance orchestras or to a big-name national band such as the Glenn Miller Orchestra or the Dorsey Brothers.

Lights were put around Halstad's ball field in 1952 and for a couple of summers thereafter, a town-team baseball game was part of the Saturday evening revelry. Attendance at ballgames sometimes reached close to 1,000. Baseball fans from miles around added even more spice to Halstad Saturday nights.

With the bustling activity, the phrase, "out on the town on Saturday night" had as much meaning in Halstad, Minnesota during the early 1950s as it has anytime, anywhere. The scene was repeated in nearly every town in the area.

The early 1950s were, in many ways, the glory years of the small town. Although the underlying economic facts were sobering—most importantly, that farms were already increasing in size and efficiency—nobody noticed but the pencil-pushing, pencil-necked government officials who kept track of that sort of thing. More Halstad young were leaving after graduation than were staying, but they were still being replaced in more than adequate numbers for the town to maintain the appearance of vigor. The vocational choices of the youth might have been construed as a subtle warning sign. Very few of the graduates of 1952 were destined to stay in Halstad, and many of them took up careers that wouldn't have allowed them to stay if they had wanted. The rush to the suburbs and large regional centers that would eventually drain the small town of people in the prime of their careers was on.

In 1950, only a prophet, or maybe a good demographer, would have seen the decline coming. It has been said that a prophet is never welcome in his home town, and for good reason: Prophets just ruin the fun. No matter what the future held, the early 1950s were a busy and colorful time to live in a small town, and particularly in the small town of Halstad, Minnesota.

Chapter 5

Cast of Characters

Don Thompson sits upright in an armchair in the living room of his comfortable home in Mahnomen, Minnesota, visiting about the 1952 Halstad basketball team. The tallest member of the team at just over six feet, Thompson was the starting center. Talk soon turns to the team's coach, Ray Kerrigan.

"Kerrigan," Thompson said, gesturing at his living room, "is the reason we have all this."

Don Thompson grew up in grinding poverty and, unlike most people of modest means at the time, he knew it. His father worked long hours to provide for five children on a farm laborer's wage. Although the Thompsons moved into the town of Halstad when Don was in elementary school, their house was small and unpretentious. Don Thompson never felt as if he became a town kid. Elementary school taunts of "dumb country kid" stuck with him for many years.

Then, along came Ray Kerrigan. Kerrigan needed a center for his basketball team, and Don Thompson was the tallest boy around. Although he had no particular talent for basketball when Kerrigan found him, Thompson was an athlete. Kerrigan worked with Thompson for hours at a time for years, teaching him to pivot both ways and shoot with his left hand as well as he could shoot with his right. More importantly to Don Thompson today, Ray Kerrigan taught him to believe that he could succeed. Off the court, Thompson might have felt like a dumb country kid—shy, awkward, poor—but on the court, thanks to Ray Kerrigan, "I felt I belonged."

"Kerrigan instilled in you the belief that if you wanted something, you just had to go out and get it," Thompson said. "That stuck with me." And the one thing Don Thompson wanted to do in life was to get out of poverty.

Kerrigan also emphasized that college was the way out of poverty. Thompson, like the others of Halstad's Starting Five, went to college and became a teacher. He didn't stop there. While teaching full-time, Thompson, with the help of his wife Jane, started an accounting firm which at its peak served 300 clients. For good measure, he and a friend started a construction firm. The house, the "all this" that Don Thompson credited to Ray Kerrigan, was designed by Thompson and built with his own hands.

Don Thompson was not as natural a basketball player as teammates Darrel Hesby and Jimmy Akason, and he didn't possess their town-kid confidence. But inspired by Ray Kerrigan, Don not only became a force on the court, but went on to achieve his life's goals through determination and hard work. Don Thompson will be the first to tell you that basketball—and Ray Kerrigan—changed his life.

Ray Kerrigan and the town of Halstad were an odd pair. A gregarious, volatile Irishman with charisma flowing out his ears, Kerrigan turned heads in Halstad with his manner.

"He had an air about him," said a former player. "I don't know if it was cockiness, arrogance, or what, but he had an air about him."

To be described as having an air about you is not a compliment in a stoic Norwegian farm town. To stand out from others in any way—whether by being loud, or by excelling, or by not excelling, or by talking too much—is to invite stares, comments and, at worst, the silent treatment.

But when Ray Kerrigan came to Halstad in 1948, he had an advantage. He already knew how to deal with stoic Norwegian Lutherans.

Like most Irishmen, Ray's father was Catholic. Ray's mother was a dour English Anglican, but the Kerrigan family, who lived in a small town in southern Minnesota called Houston, was Catholic, the story goes, until Ray's father, who himself had a temper, had a disagreement with the priest and kicked him out of the house. From that day forward, Ray Kerrigan and the entire Kerrigan family were Lutheran.

Ray Kerrigan attended St. Olaf college, an institution so Lutheran and so Norwegian that Norway's royal family pays occasional visits. And Ray's wife, Caroline, was a Norwegian from the small town of Portland, North Dakota. So by the time Ray Kerrigan arrived in the Norwegian town of Halstad, after two years of teaching and coaching in his wife's hometown of Portland, he had perfected the difficult art of living with stoic Scandinavians. His strategy: Charm their socks off.

"A smile and a cigarette," said former Halstad ballplayer Dale Serum, "Ray always had a smile and a cigarette."

Kerrigan jumped into his duties in Halstad with enthusiasm and verve. He was principal, but he also taught whatever class needed teaching, be it biology, chemistry, history, or physics. "I am sure there were topics when he was just one day ahead of the kids," said his daughter Karen.

Even though he never played basketball, baseball or football, Kerrigan coached all three. There was simply nobody else qualified to do the job.

Kerrigan was aware of his role as principal in the little town of Halstad. Teachers were not to go to the bar. Teachers were not to even drink in their own homes. A principal was not only expected to join the big church in town, he was to become a church leader.

Ray Kerrigan was a stickler for appropriateness. He took his various roles seriously. He saved his nipping for fishing trips or for infrequent trips to Fargo to the Nestor Lounge with a couple of his buddies. Meanwhile, he spearheaded the church building project. He even taught church school classes.

But Kerrigan was no goody-goody. He smoked constantly. He told off-color jokes. His language could be salty, at least around the boys.

Kerrigan simultaneously cultivated both sides of the tracks in Halstad. Pastor Carl Opsahl couldn't argue with him, for Kerrigan volunteered for every church project there was. The town leaders loved Kerrigan because he volunteered for their projects as well and was great fun to be around. The boys down at the bar couldn't find fault with Kerrigan, for although he couldn't sit down and drink with them, he could entertain them with ribald stories and impress them with his take-no-prisoners approach to coaching. Kerrigan's charisma won over the town.

"Everybody loved Ray," people still say to this day, even those who thought him a little rough around the edges. That love and respect arose because underneath it all, under the roughness and toughness and behind the clouds of cigarette smoke, people correctly sensed that Ray Kerrigan cared about every student in his school, every player on his teams, and every person he ran into on the streets of Halstad. He was, at bottom, a softie.

A strange thing about Ray Kerrigan: Although he had Ted Williams' good looks, a winning smile, a booming voice, an intimidating glare, and a reasonably impressive frame, Kerrigan always let his curly brown hair grow into an unmanageable mop. His hair was unruly at a time when crew cuts were the rage, years before long hair was a sign of rebellion.

At a game in Mahnomen, Kerrigan overheard a girl in the stands say to her friend, "I just wish I could cut off that Halstad coach's hair!" Kerrigan pulled out his pocket knife, turned around to the girl and said, "Would this work?"

The story behind Kerrigan's mop, a feature he

maintained to his death, goes back to his infancy, according to his daughter Karen.

Ma and Pa Kerrigan had a plan for their family from the beginning of their marriage. That in itself was odd, since family planning was pretty haphazard during the 1910s. But they decided that they would have three children three years apart and that would be it.

The couple pulled it off. Three sons, William, Beryl, and Charles were born three years apart. No more children were on the horizon—until tragedy struck.

One spring day in 1916, Ma Kerrigan was baking cookies. She gave a fresh chocolate chip cookie to little Charlie and sent him outside to eat it on the back step. As Ma returned to her baking, she heard the dog let out a horrible whine. She went out back to see what was the matter. Charles was gone. The dog was looking down the well. Little Charles had drowned at three-and-a-half years of age.

Ma Kerrigan would never recover from the loss of her baby boy. But Ma and Pa Kerrigan decided to have one more child. And so Ray Kerrigan was born on January 9, 1917. To the grief-stricken Ma Kerrigan, baby Ray became the little girl she had never had.

She dressed Ray in baby girl's clothing. She kept him

inside. She didn't let him rough-house with the other little boys. And she never let him cut his hair short.

When Ray went to school, the girl's clothing obviously had to go. And after he was teased mercilessly, his brothers took him to the barber over a noon hour and had his locks cut off. But his hair soon grew back, and Ray continued to be his mother's favorite.

As Ray grew into boyhood, he continued to stay inside and help his mother. She didn't allow him to play sports. Instead, he read, helped with the housework, and developed an interest in music. When Ray Kerrigan went to college, rather than play sports, he played trumpet in St. Olaf's legendary band.

The bond between Ray Kerrigan and his mother remained strong until his death. Although others found Ma Kerrigan sour to the point of stand-offish, Ray worshipped the ground she walked on, even writing poems in her honor well into his adulthood.

As his career developed and Ray Kerrigan became ever busier with teaching, coaching, and endless community projects, he maintained one habit. Every Sunday evening, he rolled a sheet of paper in the old typewriter on his desk at home. Every night before he went to bed, he painstakingly typed with the index finger on each hand a summary of his day on that piece of paper. At the end of the week, he signed the letter, folded it up and mailed it to his mother.

So that is the story of Ray Kerrigan's hair. He kept it long because he knew his mother wanted it that way.

It is possible that Ray Kerrigan's rather odd upbringing contributed to another quirk, as well. He was fond of pink socks, and sometimes wore them to the ballgames he coached.

Ma Kerrigan's refusal to let little Ray play sports meant that Kerrigan never participated in any of the sports he would eventually coach with such distinction. In fact, Ray Kerrigan knew very little about sports. But Ray Kerrigan knew how to motivate men, a lesson he was to learn the hard way.

After graduating from St. Olaf College, Kerrigan was hired to teach at Augustana Academy, a private high school in Canton, South Dakota. There he met Caroline. They fell in love. There was just one problem: Caroline was a student.

Because she had stayed home to care for her ailing mother before returning to high school at age 19, Caroline was older than the other students. But that did little to mollify the administration at Augustana when

Ray, a teacher, and Caroline, a student, were seen holding hands on campus.

Kerrigan survived the severe reprimand for the hand-holding incident, but then World War II broke out. He enlisted in the Naval Air Corps and was sent to Pensacola, Florida, for training. Like thousands of young couples, Ray and Caroline decided to get married. Caroline and Ma Kerrigan took a train from Minnesota to Florida for the wedding. On the way, Caroline called ahead to Ray to ask if he could find a nice girl to be her maid-of-honor.

"I wasn't that stupid," Ray Kerrigan said years later. Instead of finding a girl to fill the maid-of-honor position, he leaned on a buddy named Morris Birchfield. Maid-of-honor Mr. Birchfield became a life-long family friend.

Not so with Ray Kerrigan's best man, a flier named Kalish from Breckenridge, Minnesota. A few days after the Kerrigans' wedding in Pensacola, Kalish's plane went down in a training mission and he was killed. Ray Kerrigan's searing experience with war-time reality began with a jarring thud.

After the wedding, Caroline went back north. Ray Kerrigan served four years, first training pilots in math, science, and navigation, later flying B-24 sub-chasers himself.

First he flew missions from Florida up the coast to Maine, bombing suspected German U-boats and then making passes to look for the oil slicks which would indicate a direct hit. If the sub surfaced, you had to finish it off. Kerrigan found the work grim. Sometimes you came close to hitting your own. Other times the German subs would break surface and their crewmen would flip the B-24s the bird.

Eventually, Kerrigan was shipped to the Mediterranean where he bombed German U-boats on runs from Africa to Gibraltar. The heavy, humid weather in that part of the world was inimical to the B-24, and Kerrigan had many close calls. Once, while attempting a landing at night on an airstrip in England, Kerrigan was forced to pull up after branches from a grove of trees beat against the plane's belly.

The four years in the military toughened up Ray Kerrigan and made him a leader of men. He learned when to explode and when to cajole. He worked to figure out which of his airmen he could kick in the butt and which he had to sit down with for a heart-to-heart talk. If he didn't know before, he learned in the Army how to be one of the boys, how to swear, how to smoke, how to tell a dirty story.

Like many veterans of World War II, Ray Kerrigan didn't spend a lot of time after the war talking about his war experiences. As a classroom teacher, he was fond of drifting from the subject at hand, but seldom did he mention the war in anything but vague terms. Yet, the war clearly affected him.

He was haunted by the oil slicks from sunken subs, the close calls, the loss of buddies. He never talked about the war even with his own family, and only rarely did he use war stories to directly inspire his teams. But when Ray Kerrigan had a chance to use the sometimes harsh leadership methods he mastered in the war for the less urgent matter of coaching, he didn't hesitate.

Kerrigan believed in the importance of rules. If you were in Ray Kerrigan's charge, you obeyed the rules. Obeying the rules built character. You did not question the validity of the rules, for their validity was not important. What was important was bending to rules for the sake of rules. Learning to obey the rules meant you could be depended upon to do the right thing when the going got tough. Kerrigan applied a well-defined set of rules to his teams and to the entire school. His rule-heavy approach fit the times well.

Kerrigan's coaching methods would not pass muster

today. When he once called a time-out only to have two of his players gaze up in the stands towards their girlfriends, Ray Kerrigan grabbed them by the hair and bonked their heads together so hard that both saw stars—this in front of a gym full of people. When mild-mannered, hard-working Don Thompson put in a sluggish first half, Kerrigan grabbed him in the locker room at half-time, turned him around, and literally kicked him in the butt as hard as he could.

Kerrigan could lose his temper on the sidelines, although he didn't hassle the referees. One time, he was so upset with his team that he tried to call a time-out. When he failed to get the attention of the players, he stormed up to the head table and pushed the buzzer to stop the game. The referees blew the whistle but were too surprised to call a technical foul.

In his first year of coaching at Halstad, Kerrigan smoked in the locker room at half-time. His ability to devour a cigarette was legendary. Darrel Hesby and Jimmy Akason, both on the team as ninth graders, remember watching Kerrigan inhale deeply. "No smoke came out," Hesby said. "We didn't know where it went."

"Three drags and that baby was gone," according to Jim Akason.

Later, for reasons nobody knows, Kerrigan stopped smoking in the locker room. Instead, he would give his pep talk, try to stir the boys up, then leave them to stew in their juices while he headed down to the boiler room for a smoke before the second half. After a game, it wasn't long before Kerrigan had a cigarette in his hand, sometimes when he was standing in the middle of the gym and the crowd was still clearing out. After-school basketball practice didn't start until Kerrigan arrived from the boiler room reeking of smoke.

Even after Coach Kerrigan arrived from the boiler room, practice was an informal affair. There were few designed plays to go over. At least if there were designed plays, Kerrigan didn't know them. Basketball was still in its adolescence, its strategies primitive by today's standards. The boys usually came up with their own. Mere motivation, at which Kerrigan excelled, counted for more than it does today.

Kerrigan did insist upon conditioning. The players jumped a lot of rope during practice, which Don Thompson credited for his eventual ability to jump 30 inches in the air. And as practice ended—and it always had to end in time for the boys to get home for six o'clock supper—Kerrigan passed out multi-vitamins to all.

Today, Kerrigan's former players agree that he wasn't an Xs and Os man. He didn't have a great knowledge of the game of basketball, and even less so of baseball. What Kerrigan did have was an intimate knowledge of human nature. He was a master psychologist, an inspirational leader. He was lucky to inherit a formidable batch of talented athletes when he came to Halstad, athletes who had trained themselves in the basics of the sports he coached. But the athletes were lucky to have happened upon the tutelage of Ray Kerrigan, a man who knew just how to milk them for all they were worth.

Ray Kerrigan acknowledged to anybody who would listen that he didn't know much about the game of basketball. His disclaimers were printed in the big-city newspapers whenever Halstad made it to the big time. They weren't taken seriously, and for good reason. An article published by the *Minneapolis Tribune* in 1952 contained a startling statistic: For the first five years Ray Kerrigan was coach at Halstad High School, 1948-1952, the very glory years of Minnesota basketball, no coach in the state had a better record than he did. He was handed talented players, no doubt, but it is also certain that Ray Kerrigan knew how to coach a team.

When Kerrigan took over Halstad's basketball team for the 1948-1949 season, he inherited a young man who was already a star, Martin Akason's son Jimmy. For that matter, Coach Kerrigan also inherited Martin Akason. Martin sensed early on that his son would be something special on the basketball court, and he wasn't going to leave his development to chance. Like most crop farmers, Martin Akason had winters free, so he lingered in the shadows of the Halstad gym during nearly every basketball practice. There was never any sense that he was unwelcome. Other locals such as Erwin Warner showed up as well. But it was obvious to all that Martin Akason took Jimmy's basketball career more seriously than any of the other fathers.

Jimmy Akason grew up in a hurry. By age eight he was on the tractor by himself tilling his father's fields. It wasn't long after that Martin Akason noticed that his son could shoot a basketball. And the kid was growing like a weed.

Martin Akason decided that it might be good for young Jimmy to attend the premier Minnesota sporting event of the day, the Minnesota State Boys Basketball Tournament at Williams Arena in St. Paul. It was 1945. Martin had to convince his wife Esther to let Jimmy go to the tournament. Young Jimmy overheard his father say, "The kid works like a hired man, he deserves a trip."

Martin won the day. He took Jimmy to the station in Moorhead, handed him a hotel reservation, tickets to the state tournament games, his return ticket, and some cash and put him on the train. Jimmy Akason was ten years old.

He was accompanied on the trip by Roger Onsgaard, age fourteen, son of the Ford dealer in Halstad. Together, they made the long train trip to Minneapolis, a city which to that point in her life Jimmy's mother Esther had never even visited.

The State Boys Basketball Tournament at the time was the biggest sporting event in Minnesota—bar none. It drew over 75,000 fans to old Williams Arena for the three-day affair. Tickets were sold out months in advance. And from 1945 through 1952, Jimmy Akason didn't miss a single game.

In 1946, Halstad School hired a new superintendent, Arnold Kittleson. Kittleson was a model of professionalism and competence, and when he heard that Martin Akason planned to take his son out of school to send him to the state tournament, he became alarmed. After some effort, Kittleson found Martin Akason uptown at the barbershop. With young Jimmy in the barber's chair, Kittleson sat down next to Martin Akason and said, "You mean to tell me you are sending an eleven-year-old boy down to Minneapolis to see the state tournament by himself?"

"He went last year," Martin Akason responded. That was the end of the discussion.

Jimmy Akason was a big kid when he was ten years old and went to the tournament for the first time, as big as the fourteen-year-old Roger Onsgaard who accompanied him. He continued to outgrow his classmates by leaps and bounds. By the time he was in the 8th grade, Jimmy Akason had a full beard and had reached his final height of five-foot-eleven-and-a-half. From eighth grade on, he started on the varsity team.

By the eighth grade, Jim Akason also had full use of the booming, baritone voice that he inherited from his father. Without even realizing it, Jimmy used that voice to command the basketball floor. With his basketball talent, his dignified bearing, and that wonderful voice, there was never any question that when Jimmy Akason was on the floor, he was in charge.

Despite his son's prodigious talents and early achievements, Martin Akason wasn't easily satisfied. He clearly wanted Jimmy to improve all the time. Martin attended most practices, as well as all the games. And he sat Jimmy down at the kitchen table after each event to dissect his performance. The other players were aware that Jimmy Akason, who towered above them in so many ways, didn't have the easiest time of it when he got home.

"I learned early on that the coach was the boss," Jim Akason says today. "Dad never made negative comments about the coach. Never. But he did make comments about me!"

Martin Akason's interest in Jimmy's career sometimes went beyond the usual bounds. In ninth grade during a varsity game against Twin Valley, Jimmy Akason ran up an amazing point total. He reached 32 by the third quarter, this at a time when teams didn't often score over 50 points in an entire game. The Minnesota State record at that time, to the extent that they kept track, was 38. Jimmy was a cinch to snatch the record at the age of fourteen.

Martin Akason would have none of it. As the story goes, he bolted out of the stands, walked straight up to Ray Kerrigan and said, "Get him out of there!" Kerrigan complied. Thus, the best game of Jimmy Akason's career ended in the third quarter with his point total stalled at 32.

Perhaps Martin Akason thought fourteen was too early for a young man to own the state scoring record.

Maybe he thought it would go to the kid's head. Perhaps he feared repercussions if his boy ran up the score against an overmanned Twin Valley team. But you have to wonder what Jimmy Akason might have done that night had he been left in the game.

As a sophomore, Akason was nominated as one of the five outstanding athletes in the WDAY listening area. Ray Kerrigan brought him to Fargo for the banquet. Peggy Lee was the entertainment. Over fifty athletes attended with their coaches. Although Jim Akason finished second in the voting to an athlete from Valley City, North Dakota, what he remembered most about the evening was the conversation he had with Ray Kerrigan on the way down to Fargo. Kerrigan told Akason of his hopes for him. It was one of the few times the two had talked at any length.

Akason went on to score 1,640 points in his high school career. That statistic wasn't uncovered until a sports reporter called Ray Kerrigan over ten years after Jim Akason graduated.

"Could you go through the books", the reporter asked, "and find out Akason's actual career total?"

Kerrigan did. When the resulting list of all-time scoring leaders in Minnesota was published, Akason looked it over and discovered that although he hadn't known it at the time, he had been Minnesota's all-time leading scorer from 1952 until his scoring record was broken in 1956.

Jimmy Akason's best buddy was Darrel Hesby. From elementary school, Jimmy and Darrel ran together around town. From playing basketball in Grandma Hesby's living room to shooting baskets in the middle of the night when it was below zero outside the Akason's rented house, to propping the door open to the coal chute at school so they could sneak in to play in a darkened gym on Saturday mornings, to outright walking up to the superintendent's house early Saturday morning to ask for the gym keys, Darrel and Jimmy did whatever it took to play ball. The superintendent at the time, possibly admiring the kids' persistence, once threw the keys at the boys and growled, "Bring 'em back when you're done."

Both Darrel Hesby and Jimmy Akason could shoot. Both were fast. The comparisons end there, for in many ways, Hesby and Akason were like oil and water. Muscular Jimmy Akason had movie star good looks from eighth grade on, while slight Darrel Hesby wore horn-rimmed glasses and looked like the winner of the science fair. Akason had a big voice and a booming laugh, while Hesby's voice was a bit squeaky and his laugh an impish giggle. Akason inspired admiration in opponents, while

Hesby, for some reason, irritated opponents and their fans to the point of distraction.

Perhaps it was Hesby's attitude. When Jimmy Akason acted self-assured, people lauded his confidence. When Darrel Hesby acted equally self-assured, people thought he was cocky.

Perhaps it was Hesby's appearance. Gangly boys with horn-rimmed glasses are supposed to sit on the end of the bench and come in during the fourth quarter for a few token minutes. They aren't supposed to be the best shooter on the floor. They aren't supposed to run circles around the opposition.

Perhaps it was Darrel Hesby's intelligence. He was generally the smartest player on the floor, exploiting the weaknesses of the opponent, showing up at the right place at the right time, being generally "shifty," to quote an archrival town's newspaper. It didn't seem right that Hesby, so thin, so gangly, so intellectual, could so completely outplay more likely-looking athletes. Or, perhaps it was Hesby's slowness getting up off the floor after he was knocked down. Oh my, it was a production for Hesby to pull himself together and get up.

"He always would act like he was half-killed," according to one spectator. Whether he was trying to draw a foul or whether he authentically felt injured, Hesby's act earned him jeers from the opposing crowd.

Both Darrel Hesby and Jim Akason preferred to have the ball in their own hands. That was apparent to all who watched them play. Sometimes it became a problem, and at least once Kerrigan sat them both down so they could see that others could shoot as well. Jimmy Akason, however, was smart enough not to put his desire to hang onto the ball in words. Darrel Hesby, meanwhile, made no bones about the fact that he didn't like to inbound the ball because he knew he might not see it again during that trip up the court.

But Darrel Hesby could shoot, and he could run. Together, he and Jimmy Akason developed into a formidable tandem by the time they were sophomores at Halstad High.

It was radio which made Jimmy Akason's name well-known in northwestern Minnesota and eastern North Dakota. To this day, people above a certain age for about a hundred-and-fifty-mile radius show a flash of recognition when they hear the name Jimmy Akason. In fact, Jimmy Akason was probably better known in Northwestern Minnesota than was the great Minnesota Laker, George Mikan. The reason? Virtually all newspaper sports reporting at the time was local. Virtually all sports broadcasts on the radio were also local. Minnesota had only one professional big league team, the Minneapolis Lakers, and their broadcasts did not reach as far north as the Red River Valley. The national sports media networks were undeveloped, and national sports games seldom reached local radio outlets.

What did come over the radio during the dark months of winter on the prairie were local basketball games. Once the Pirates showed promise, the Halstad merchants sponsored the broadcast of almost every away game—and most of Halstad's games were played on the road, thanks to Ray Kerrigan's willingness to drive almost any distance to find a challenging opponent. Usually, the broadcast came over KROX in Crookston with Jerry Dahlberg announcing. Less frequently, Manny Marget of KVOX in Moorhead, or Bill Weaver of WDAY in Fargo would feature a Halstad game as the game of the week.

Due to frequent radio coverage, the Halstad team, despite coming from a school which sometimes graduated fewer than twenty, was well known for a hundred miles around. Once they started winning big in 1949, Halstad actually developed a regional following—at least among those who didn't have a good team of their own.

The radio broadcasts increased the enthusiasm of the home town for its teams. To little Clarence Stennes, hearing the basketball team on the radio put the players on equal footing with The Lone Ranger. He was in awe that he could see his heroes walking the hallways of the Halstad School the next morning. According to Jim Akason, one of the heroes on par with the Lone Ranger, "You could tell walking down the street who had listened to the game the night before by how they looked at you."

Changes in rules made basketball more exciting. Free throws were limited to fouls. The center jump after each basket was done away with. New coaching philosophies also helped. The game now emphasized big men and the fast break. As a result, basketball was much more exciting to watch in the late 1940s than it had been only ten years before.

Changes in the times—World War II was over, as was the Great Depression—and changes in farming meant that the people of Minnesota had more time to watch basketball. With television's reach still limited to the city, a basketball game was the most exciting option on a cold winter's night in the small town.

In Halstad, zest for basketball was as strong as anywhere in Minnesota. The Pirates were a joy to watch.

Under Ray Kerrigan's coaching and Jimmy Akason's leadership on the floor, Halstad adopted an exciting brand of fast break offense. It is no wonder that tickets to basketball games in Halstad's 1939 WPA gymnasium were difficult to find. People stood in line an hour before games. During the peak seasons of the early 1950s, the school sold season tickets as soon as the basketball schedule was released in the fall.

The only thing else to do in the winter was skate on the river. Boys basketball was the only game in town. Women's basketball had been banned. Halstad was too small to have hockey or to put a wrestling team on the mat. And television was still one year away. Crop farmers didn't have much to do in the winter and were eager to get out of the house. A basketball game was as good an excuse as any.

Another factor contributed to the mania: School consolidation in the early 1950s had reached a stage where everybody who said they were from Halstad attended the Halstad school or sent their children there. Before that, many people who lived in the Halstad area went to country school and never made it to the big school in town. They had nothing to do with the high school, and didn't necessarily identify with its sports teams. And after the early 1950s, consolidation marched on to the point where neighboring towns combined into hyphenated combinations with new nicknames. Rivals Hendrum and Halstad eventually combined to become the Norman County West Panthers.

But in the early 1950s, Halstad was Halstad, Hendrum was Hendrum, and a definite line separated the two. If you said you were from Halstad, you went into Halstad on Saturday nights to get your groceries, shop, and visit with other Halstad residents. You also were probably a member of one of the Halstad area Lutheran churches served by Rev. Carl Opsahl. Perhaps at no point in Halstad's history, or in the history of small town Minnesota, were small towns and their surrounding farms more closely knit and as united in their identity as they were in the golden years of the early 1950s.

As the mania for basketball grew, capacity crowds in Halstad and the other tiny gyms in northwestern Minnesota became the norm. Often the auditoriums had to be locked half an hour before the game to prevent overcrowding. During cold weather, the humidity generated by the crowd in the gym would condense on the ceiling and rain down on the floor, making conditions dangerously slippery. Spectators' feet stuck out onto the court, sometimes tripping the referees. Players would complete a layup only to find themselves skidding across a stage. Lighting was atrocious. In Waubun's gymnasium, the lights were so dim that the Halstad players would sit in the locker room with the lights off to get their eyes adjusted before going out to play the game. In Glyndon, shots taken from the free-throw line with a normal arc would deflect off the ceiling.

In this heady, formative time for small town basketball, Ray Kerrigan thrived. He loved to discuss upcoming games with the locals over morning coffee at Bake Johnson's bakery. After each game, several friends would gather over at the Kerrigan house to go over every play until the wee hours. Local sports godfather Erwin Warner was never far from Kerrigan's ear. There was plenty of advice to go around, and the constant commentary never seemed to bother the gregarious Ray Kerrigan.

As principal of the school, Kerrigan had some control over who was hired to teach. Due to the popularity of town baseball at the time, it was a common practice to hire not just somebody who could coach, but somebody who could play baseball. When war veteran Larry Macleod, who had recently graduated from Mayville State University a few miles across the river from Halstad, applied for a job in 1950, Kerrigan snapped him up and made him assistant basketball coach.

After returning from the war, during which he had served as an off-shore medic on D-Day, Larry Macleod had a successful academic and athletic career at Mayville State. He could run circles around the Halstad boys on the basketball court, and he played side by side with them on the diamond during the summer. When he arrived, Macleod contributed something to the Halstad teams that Ray Kerrigan lacked—an intimate knowledge of basketball. Kerrigan was more than happy to defer to his assistant Larry Macleod on matters of Xs and Os, while the head coach maintained his command over the team's motivation and morale.

Kerrigan had worked with center sophomore Don Thompson for endless hours teaching him to pivot both ways. Now Macleod took over and showed Thompson even more moves. Thompson worked hard.

"He'd go through a wall for you," Macleod said of Thompson fifty-five years later.

When you hire a history teacher based upon his ball-playing abilities, you don't expect him to do much in the classroom. But Larry Macleod the history teacher was a stern taskmaster. Imbued with military discipline, Macleod brooked no nonsense in his Ancient History, World History and American History classes. He sometimes clashed with the kids, but he had no problem with the parents, for in Halstad at the time, the teacher was always right.

Macleod believed it, too. One time, Larry Macleod mistakenly gave his students the wrong test. Naturally, they didn't do well. Macleod expressed his dismay. When it was discovered that the test had been for the next chapter they were to cover, Macleod didn't back down.

"You still should have done better," he grumbled.

Like Kerrigan, Macleod could be rough. But while Kerrigan's childhood was merely a little odd, Macleod's was downright tough. His mother died at an early age and his father drank. Macleod was shuttled from relative to relative. He took refuge in sports, and during his sophomore year of high school at Park River, North Dakota, Macleod was named the best player in the conference.

The next year, Macleod started the season just as strongly. However, as he moved from one relative's home to another, he ended up at a remote farm without a phone—and he missed a game.

"I would have cut off both arms to get to that game," Macleod says today. But his coach had no sympathy. He figured Larry Macleod had missed the game deliberately to show how badly he was needed by the team. The coach benched Macleod over a dozen games until he finally bowed to community pressure near the end of the season and allowed Macleod to play. Macleod's junior season was ruined for what he felt was an unjust reason. He returned the next season to once again win the award as the best player in the conference, but the unjust benching during his junior season burned for years after.

As a result, when he became a coach, Macleod always gave his players the benefit of the doubt—at least until they proved they didn't deserve it. Macleod went on to become a coach, and eventually the athletic director, at Moorhead State University in Moorhead, Minnesota. Now in his eighties, he has little memory for or interest in specific games or specific seasons. What Macleod does remember vividly are the people. He spoke with pride of one quarterback he coached who is now a renowned Shakespearean scholar. He spoke with pain of a Halstad player who he felt he mishandled and caused hardship.

During his summers in Halstad, Macleod not only played on the town team, but like many ballplayers, he worked for the Rural Electric Co-op. The co-op was busy at the time. Not only had it brought power to the farms, but soon the company had to move the poles due to the widening of the roads, which started in 1951. Macleod's co-worker on the co-op crew, Erman Ueland, remembers

Macleod talking to a young boy as they worked on the electric poles near the kid's farm.

"What are your interests? How are you doing in school?"

The kid shrugged Macleod off. "I'm stupid," he said.

"Who told you that?" Macleod replied.

"Oh, my teachers tell me I'm stupid."

Macleod grabbed the boy by the shoulders, squatted down to his level, looked him in the eye, and said, "Don't let anybody tell you that you are stupid!"

In Macleod, Kerrigan found an assistant coach who shared both his toughness and his love for kids. In addition, Macleod brought to the Halstad gym a knowledge of the game of basketball and the physical ability to press the players hard in practice.

As the summer of 1951 progressed, the boys worked and played baseball. There were no summer basketball camps at that time. The boys rarely even shot baskets during the summer. When there was no snow on the ground, it was all baseball in Halstad, and lots of it. If you add up the number of games they played for the high school team, the town team, the Jaycee's team, and the Legion team, many of boys played over seventy competitive baseball games that summer. When they weren't playing an opponent, Erwin Warner would hold practice.

Jimmy Akason was the shortstop. Hesby played the outfield. Morrie Holm pitched. Dale Serum caught. Only Don Thompson of the basketball's Starting Five, whose throwing arm was ruined when the crank on a tractor kicked back on him as a young boy, stayed off the diamond.

As summer drew to a close, the baseball season wound down, and school approached, Jimmy Akason, Darrel Hesby, and Dale Serum jumped in the car one late August day and drove up to the town of Shelly, six miles north, to chase girls. It is a time honored-tradition in small towns: The girls are prettier in the next town, and the boys are more handsome. On this lazy, late-summer day, nothing much came of their trip. The boys returned to Halstad late in the afternoon and stopped at the cafe for a bite to eat.

As the boys walked into the cafe, a grim-faced local came up to Jimmy Akason and said, "Jim, you are wanted at home."

Martin Akason was dead. He had died that afternoon while sitting in his living room chair.

Chapter 6

Building a Team

The death of Martin Akason of a heart attack at fifty-two years of age hit Halstad hard. The loss of the big man with the big voice left a conspicuous hole, particularly when that man was basketball star Jimmy Akason's father. To little basketball fan Clarence Stennes, about to enter the fifth grade, Martin Akason's death was the first time it ever occurred to him that somebody's dad might die.

Esther Akason was left with two boys and a crop in the field. When it came time to harvest the sugar beets, the town pitched in. Seventy-eight farmers showed up on a late September day with machinery in tow. They removed the entire crop of 673 tons of beets from the Akason farm in one day using 22 trucks. Fifty-six women served the crew a ham dinner. The proceeds from the one-day harvest helped Esther pay some of the farm debts.

Jimmy Akason, who already had grown up in a hurry, was now the man of the house. Because Martin Akason had rented the land he farmed, liquidating the assets wasn't difficult. And there was never any question of Jimmy Akason taking over the farm. Esther, who had a college education, wanted Jimmy to go to college. And it was clear to Jim that farming, aside from being a lot of hard work, was not the way to procure a stable income.

Some time after the funeral, Jimmy, now a high school senior, went to the bank with his mother to help settle Martin's financial matters. The banker who helped them was Norman Aamot. As Jimmy and Esther sat across the desk from Aamot, he sympathized with their plight. His wife had cancer and had been given a month to live.

Aamot's wife passed away within a few weeks. A few months later, the banker proposed to Esther. Jimmy Akason was relieved that his mother, still a young woman of forty-two, was going to be taken care of.

So, it was a tumultuous year for Jimmy Akason off the court and off the field, and there was little reason to expect him to have the most successful sports season of his long career during those same few months.

Instead of his father in the stands and in the shadows at practice, Jimmy's uncle Clarence Akason took on the supporting role. After Martin Akason's death, his brother Clarence didn't miss a game, even though he lived a dozen miles across the river in North Dakota. Unlike his brother Martin, Clarence didn't offer criticisms of Jimmy after the practices and the games. More than a few Halstad fans noticed that Jimmy Akason was more relaxed on the basketball floor his senior season than he had been before the tragic loss of his father. Perhaps basketball was a good outlet for a kid who had a lot on his mind.

The 1952 Halstad basketball team was years in the making. The Starting Five were all seniors in 1952, but they all had ample varsity experience. Jimmy Akason was a five-year veteran by his senior year. Darrel Hesby wasn't far behind, having four years of experience playing on the A squad. Don Thompson had started at center since his sophomore season. Morrie Holm didn't come out for basketball until his sophomore year, but his natural athleticism allowed him to improve in a hurry and start on varsity as a junior. Dale Serum matured late, but by the time he was a senior, he had reached his full height and weight.

Jimmy Akason dominated Halstad's attack as early as the ninth grade. He was fourteen, but already well-known for his ability to command on the floor. The high scoring game of his career, when he scored 32 points against Twin Valley before Kerrigan removed him in the second half, came during that ninth grade season. The box scores of other games during early 1949 show that Akason regularly scored more than 20 points, this at a time when scores of 32-29 weren't unusual.

Ninth-grader Darrel Hesby frequently started as well. Although his scoring totals didn't match his friend Jimmy Akason's, Hesby's shifty play and nifty shooting were from early on a part of Halstad's attack.

The 1949 Halstad team finished second in the district tournament, the first time any Halstad basketball team had made it that far. That year, Halstad's sedate newspaper, the Valley Journal Review, began to cover basketball like it had never done before. In Jimmy Akason, the team had a legitimate star. Crowds at the Halstad gym increased to the point where school officials instituted a season-ticket plan.

Ray Kerrigan knew he had a good batch of athletes on his hands. His problem: Finding opponents to schedule who would give Halstad a run for their money. A handful of teams could compete with Halstad, but otherwise the conference schedule was somewhat soft. No doubt Erwin Warner and Kerrigan discussed the matter during their late-night bull sessions at the Kerrigan house, or at the cafe over early morning coffee. Kerrigan resolved to drive his team almost anywhere in search of worthy opponents.

The scheduling problem was exacerbated by the reluctance of large town teams to play a little school like Halstad.

"Big schools have everything to lose and nothing to gain from playing a small school," Kerrigan explained to a newspaper. "No wonder they won't schedule us."

Then number-one fan Erwin Warner made a move which was to have long-term consequences for the Halstad team. Although the large town of Thief River Falls was eighty miles north of Halstad, and its school was nearly ten times the size of Halstad's, Warner had a connection to the Thief River Falls basketball coach Bob Nick. Warner's mother was a Nick, and at Warner's urging Kerrigan arranged with his cousin for Halstad to start the season in Thief River Falls in December of 1949. It was a scheduling coup for Kerrigan and the first time Halstad had played a team from such a large school.

To soften the resistance of the larger schools, Kerrigan often offered to play them on their home courts—every year if they insisted. After 1950, the Pirates barely played one-third of their games at home due to Kerrigan's determination to add talented teams to Halstad's schedule. Thief River Falls was often on Halstad's calendar, but the game was always held in the big gym in Thief River. Halstad played Fosston many years in a row, but all the games were in Fosston—again the product of Kerrigan's willingness to drive to find quality opponents for his team.

Thief River Falls was a hockey town at the time and the early 1950s produced some of the best hockey teams in its history. At the same time, the Prowlers had a group of basketball players coming up through the ranks who, like Halstad's, were young, talented, and had played ball together since childhood. Unlike Halstad, they had several players over six feet tall. By 1952, expectations for the Thief River team were as great as they were for Halstad.

But Kerrigan had the boys hepped up for their first game ever against the Prowlers in December of 1949. The Pirates relished playing on Thief River's regulation-sized court, which suited their running game well. Thief River's big man, six-foot-five sophomore Roger Williamson, was on the shelf regaining his eligibility after spending a year at Grand Forks Central High School. With Akason and Hesby leading the way, Halstad shocked Thief River Falls in their big WPA-built gym, nicknamed "the Brick House," by 1 point when Morrie Holm sank a free throw with only a few seconds remaining. Akason and Hesby led the scoring. The victory was a widely-reported upset.

"That was when we knew we could do something," Darrel Hesby said. "Beating Thief River in 1949 was a landmark for us."

For the next few years, at least, there was no way Thief River Falls could take Halstad off its schedule without looking like they were afraid of losing to the pesky Pirates.

Not only was it a landmark win, but the victory in the Brick House started the Pirates on an incredible 14-game winning streak. With a hustling team dominated by sophomores, Halstad created a mild sensation. As the streak continued, telegrams of congratulations came in from former Halstadites all around the country, proud of the tiny school from which they had graduated. One former resident requested tickets so he could drive 250 miles to watch Halstad play archrival Ada.

Halstad's streak generated enough press to get the attention of WDAY Radio's Bill Weaver. He made the 110-mile trip from station headquarters in Fargo, North Dakota, to Fosston, Minnesota to broadcast the Halstad-Fosston game as WDAY's game-of-the-week. When you consider that there were probably fifty other games to choose from which were closer to Fargo and which involved bigger schools, it is obvious that Halstad had made its mark.

The Fosston Greyhounds made their mark, too. The Pirates' fourteen-game win streak ended in the Fosston's fancy, double-decker gymnasium. The score was Fosston 65, Halstad 63, a high-scoring game for the time. For Halstad, Jimmy Akason scored 23 and Darrel Hesby sank 15 points. Fosston was led by its star, Whitey Roysland, who scored 20. Both teams featured a fast-break offense unusual for the time. Bill Weaver was impressed by the fast pace and torrid scoring, calling it the finest high school game he had ever seen.

At the time, WDAY recorded the games and played them tape-delayed following the evening news. After the seventy-mile trip home back to Halstad, Darrel Hesby stumbled into Grandma Hesby's dining room about midnight to find his Grandfather listening to Bill Weaver broadcasting the game on the radio.

"What are you doing here?" Grandpa Hesby inquired, completely confused.

"The game is over," Darrel said. "We lost by 2."

Grandpa Hesby waved his hand in disgust and went to bed. He couldn't understand why he had wasted his time listening to a game that was already over.

Halstad won its final three games of 1950 against lesser opponents to finish the season with a conference title and a 17-1 record, only to falter early in the tournaments. But their spectacular season, during which the Pirates were led by two star sophomores in Hesby and Akason, and one developing star sophomore, Don Thompson, raised expectations for the next two seasons. It was about this time the *Fargo Forum* began to refer to the Pirates as "the vaunted Halstad team." The newspapermen had their eye on this young team, just as they were already charmed by Halstad's fiery coach, Ray Kerrigan.

The town was behind its team, for the boys on the court were earning the previously obscure Halstad a bit of regional renown. Coach Kerrigan didn't have to keep track of his team during off hours. The townspeople did it for him. Players were to be home by 10 p.m. If they weren't, word traveled fast, and Kerrigan confronted them the next morning in school. Don Thompson's older sister sometimes stayed out after ten. More than once, Kerrigan confronted Thompson about his late hours when in fact it was his sister who had pulled in the Thompson driveway after the team curfew the night before.

Once the players were confirmed, they were eligible to attend dances at the LRC. However, it was strongly suggested by Ray Kerrigan that the LRC was an inappropriate place for a ballplayer to spend a Saturday evening. In an odd prohibition, by modern standards, the boys were only to go on dates on Sunday afternoons.

Representing the town's dreams of glory and fame had benefits for the boys, too. In particular, it became sort of a contest to see which local bigwig could treat the team to a steak dinner. Erwin Warner usually won, but other townspeople took their turn as well. Until the team's success, the boys, none of whom came from wealthy households, were unaccustomed to eating steak.

"Who knows, maybe it was only ten steak dinners total," Jim Akason said, "but it sure made an impact on us."

Despite the success of the 1949-50 team, Coach Ray Kerrigan knew two talented stars wouldn't be enough to attain his goal of a district title. Many more pieces of the puzzle had to fall together before Halstad would make its presence felt in the tournaments. The team had yet to develop the uncanny balance which would launch it to success in 1952.

New assistant coach Larry Macleod worked with center Don Thompson before practice and after practice. A star on the football field, Thompson lacked the early basketball experience of Akason and Hesby. Macleod did his best to give him that experience, and unlike Kerrigan, Macleod could show Thompson the moves on the floor.

The 1950-51 team was dominated by juniors, but

two seniors played as well: Roger Stole, a forward, and guard Rod Oistad. Neither was the caliber of scorer that Jim Akason, Darrel Hesby, or Don Thompson had already become, but Oistad, the finest pitcher Halstad's baseball team ever produced, was no slouch on the basketball floor, either. When he broke a bone in his foot midway through the basketball season, it was a blow to the team's chances. But Oistad's injury also gave more playing time to underclassmen, and they benefited.

Oistad was the sixth man. He was sent in when Kerrigan wanted to talk to one of the Starting Five. That meant he sat next to Kerrigan on the bench. Kerrigan's habit of slapping the leg of the person next to him on the bench fell so hard on Oistad that Oistad's mother had to explain to others in the stands the red marks on her son's leg.

Marlyn Aanenson took advantage of increased playing time to score in double figures in several games. Morrie Holm, almost as great a pitcher on the ball diamond as his cousin Rod Oistad, used his all-around athleticism to bring the ball up the court with great speed. Relatively new to high school basketball, Holm was mature and confident in any athletic endeavor. Holm did the dirty work. He went after rebounds with ferocity, a task Darrel Hesby was too slight to attempt.

Another blue-collar fighter on the basketball floor was Dale Serum—at least by the time he was a senior. During his junior year, Serum put on a growth spurt which brought him to a solid six feet. Eventually Serum, another quiet but solid Scandinavian, could turn a game around in a few minutes with an angry burst of fast-break scoring.

Kerrigan was aware that his team, despite its successes the previous season, was a work in progress. For one thing, it wouldn't do for the team to be dependent upon Jimmy Akason and Darrel Hesby to do the bulk of the scoring. A smart opposing coach with a good plan can shut down one or two good shooters and by midway through the 1950-51 season, that is exactly what started to happen.

The 1950-1951 season began less auspiciously than the year before. Halstad started sloppily against two lesser opponents, Twin Valley and Climax. Against Twin Valley, the Pirates "nearly gave their fans heart failure," according to the paper, before pulling out a narrow win, 54-50. Against Climax, the paper said, "It looked for a time as though Kerrigan's Pirates had been caught with their weapons down."

Climax led at the half with a 20-14 lead.

"Evidently Ray Kerrigan must have whispered a few pearls of wisdom into his boys' ears because they came out fighting the second half." They went on to win 48-40. Thompson scored 18, but the second-half surge was sparked by Dale Serum, who continued to build his reputation for coming in to provide a spark when it was needed.

Kerrigan's half-time motivational tricks could involve yelling, whispering, kicking a player or two in the butt, or patting somebody on the back. After he quit smoking in the locker room in 1948, whatever half-time motivational speech he gave came before or after he disappeared for a cigarette. And sometimes, the speech revolved around his cigarette break, as happened the time the Kerrigan stormed into the locker room after an unsuccessful first half.

"You've done it your way for the first half, now figure out what you're going to do for the second," he growled and walked out for a smoke.

The 1951 season required all of Kerrigan's tricks. The team didn't jibe like they had the previous year. Fan expectations were high. Conversations at the cafe centered around what was wrong and how to fix it.

Halstad's hopes for a third consecutive conference

title took a hit when the Pirates lost to Fertile, 32-29. It was clear that Halstad's run-and-gun approach wasn't yet polished enough to penetrate a defensive-minded, ball control team. In the Fertile game, Akason was held to 12 points, Hesby and Thompson to 6 apiece.

Then came a frustrating game against Waubun. The Waubun Bombers were always a pain for Halstad. Some Halstad players attributed their difficulty with Waubun to the abysmal lighting in the Waubun gym, or to the proximity of the stage to the basket, which had the effect of discouraging players on a fast break from getting up a full head of steam on a layup. Jimmy Akason, who had more trouble with Waubun than he did with most teams, finally came to the conclusion that they were simply well-coached.

"They just knew how to defense us," he said, waving away the other excuses. "They had a good coach."

The December, 1950, game against Waubun was in Halstad. The Pirates got off to a 9-0 lead and then flopped. Waubun won in the last seconds on a basket which bounced on the rim for an extended time before it finally fell through. Waubun was no slouch, having won five games in a row at that point, but they were a team Halstad was expected to easily beat. Two consecutive defeats to conference opponents were too much for Kerrigan to bear. He decided to shake things up.

Part of the problem, Kerrigan decided, was that Jimmy Akason and Darrel Hesby still thought it was 1949, the year they led the team to a 17-1 record. Both Hesby and Akason liked to have the ball, perhaps more than they should. Both liked to shoot it, perhaps more often than was seemly. It was time, Kerrigan figured, that they learned that the rest of the team had some ability to win games as well.

So, Kerrigan benched them both. Hesby and Akason sat out the entire next game against rival Hillsboro, North Dakota, a town just a few miles across the river. As the newspaper delicately put it, Kerrigan used a "revamped lineup." The only thing revamped about it was that stars Hesby and Akason were missing. And the Pirates rolled to a lopsided 55-22 victory.

Kerrigan had driven his point home. Without its two stars, the team had, according to the newspaper, looked better than it had all season. Aggressiveness, a factor which has been conspicuous by its absence, was shown throughout the game. Not only had Kerrigan taught Hesby and Akason a lesson about team play, but the remaining players had responded by finding out that they, too, could run and gun.

Kerrigan chastened his two stars without reducing their confidence. The other players, now aware that they could handle things on their own, stepped up their play. In practice, Serum, Holm and Thompson became more aggressive, while Akason and Hesby, still secure in their positions as the established stars, saved their biggest fireworks for the games themselves. The combined styles of the players would eventually produce a team with a definite sparkle on the floor.

But not right away. Even though the team became more balanced, the 1950-51 season continued to be a tougher go than the previous year. Neighboring Ada had a good team, and handed the Pirates a third conference defeat. Fosston once again edged Halstad on their home court. And another long trip to Thief River Falls resulted in an overtime defeat 54-52 as the Prowler's ace center, Roger Williamson ran up 29 points.

Despite the setbacks, as the 1950-51 season progressed, Halstad polished the high-powered style which suited their talents.

"We played hell-bent for election," said Jim Akason.

Lacking in height, they ran hard. Once they got the ball, Holm and Serum brought it up court as if it were a race to get to the other end. Akason barked commands,

Thompson settled in under the basket—in and around the narrow six-foot wide lane of the time—and Hesby shifted around to gain position.

Such a relentless use of speed was unusual in the 1950s. By cycling in reserves, Kerrigan kept the horses fresh. Other teams, not used to the pace, simply wore down. The only problems arose when Halstad played teams with a big center.

"If they had a big guy, we couldn't get the ball back," said Akason. When a team with height played a ball-control offense, the Pirates were in trouble.

Halstad went into the tournaments of 1951 having finished third in their conference behind Fertile and Ada. After beating Clearbrook in the first round of district play, a game which featured a 26-point explosion from Darrel Hesby, Halstad finished third behind Fertile, who defeated Ada for the district title.

The high hopes Halstad had after going 17-1 when their starting line-up was made up of sophomores weren't fulfilled when the same players were juniors. However, the 1950-51 team showed improved team play. Don Thompson continued to develop at center. Holm and Serum filled out their frames and added speed and confidence. Akason and Hesby, the most naturally gifted of the players, would never again have a year like they had as sophomores. The reputation they gained that year caused other teams to key on them. What became evident throughout the 1950-51 season was that the rest of the team was becoming good enough to win even with their two stars pinned down.

Jimmy Akason had gone to the state tournament as a spectator since he was 10. Every year, more of his classmates went with him until by 1951, Kerrigan chaperoned several members of the team down to Williams Arena to see the big show. Benchwarmer guard George Allen "Squirt" Johnson remembered it well. Kerrigan and the boys were up in the coach's hotel room shooting the breeze when Kerrigan said, off-handedly, "Next year we'll come to play." Nobody took him seriously.

As the summer of 1951 proceeded, the boys played another grueling baseball schedule. Basketball wasn't on their minds. But town team baseball coach Erwin Warner's wheels were always turning. It was he who would provide the final piece of the puzzle for next year's basketball team.

Erwin Warner's sister was married to Wimpy Bernhagen. Although Wimpy was from Bird Island, Minnesota, the couple lived in Halstad. During the summer of 1951, Wimpy's brother dropped dead on the street in St. Cloud, leaving an athletically talented son to finish his school in a small town in central Minnesota with an unpromising basketball team. Erwin Warner saw opportunity and convinced the boy, Chuck Bernhagen, to come north to Halstad for his senior year.

Chuck Bernhagen had some trouble adjusting to Halstad. He stood out due to his sharp dress and his somewhat arrogant manner. He had a temper. He fought. He eventually clashed with the coaches. And he was one Catholic in a sea of Lutherans. The school cook fixed him a fish sandwich on Fridays while everybody else ate meat.

But Chuck Bernhagen gave the Halstad basketball squad another good athlete off the bench. When Akason, Thompson and Hesby were otherwise tied down, Bernhagen had the talent to bust loose for 15 points and save the day.

But, first things first. With the crisp autumn air comes football, at least in most towns. Halstad High had fielded a football team during the 1930s. After the war started, however, a couple of young men broke limbs on the football field. With so many of Halstad's young men overseas in harm's way, it seemed silly to have boys breaking legs on the cow pasture on the edge of town. So, in a concession to common sense, football was discontinued.

A few years later, with the war over, the mood changed. Jimmy Akason, Darrel Hesby, Dale Serum, Don Thompson, and several other boys loved to play football in pickup games around town. Knowing they had a probable sympathetic ear in Ray Kerrigan, they asked him to let them form a high school team. Kerrigan relented. Halstad joined a six-man football conference. Kerrigan became coach, even though his mother had never allowed him to play the game himself.

During their first season back on the gridiron, the Pirates won all four of their games. The second season, 1951, with a 190-pound Don Thompson on the line and nimble Darrel Hesby at quarterback, the Pirates won all six of their games and the conference title.

But football wasn't as popular in 1951 as it was to later become. Few spectators showed up for the games. And few mentions of the football team or its successes appeared in the Valley Journal, Halstad's somewhat hapless newspaper. When, during the football season, the upcoming season's basketball schedule was released, it merited top-of-the-front-page coverage with a large headline. It was obvious which sport was first in the hearts of Halstad sports fans.

Fortunately for the basketball fans, none of Halstad's athletes were seriously injured on the football field in the fall of 1951. As usual, school was called off for a week for potato vacation. Beet harvest was successful. Going into winter on the prairie, the townspeople wondered if the Halstad High basketball team, which had been together so many years and now was in its last year, would make the cold months shorter by finally fulfilling their high expectations.

Chapter 7

Season of Dreams

For his prized 1952 basketball team, Coach Ray Kerrigan arranged the most grueling schedule yet.

"We'll play anywhere," he told a newspaper later, and he meant it.

The first game of the year took the team 127 miles east to Bemidji where they faced a large school from Grand Rapids, Minnesota, in a tune-up for the regular season. The game was played on the 50' x 90' floor at the Bemidji State Teachers College. After leading until the final four minutes, Halstad succumbed to a last-minute barrage of 6 consecutive baskets by Grand Rapids. The final score was a modest 35-29.

Kerrigan had treated the game like a spring-training exhibition. Halstad's play was ragged. Nine players received roughly equal playing time. Jimmy Akason had only 5 points, Hesby 6. New arrival Chuck Bernhagen led the scoring for Halstad, showing quickly that he would be a vital addition to the team.

In the early 1950s, the Halstad Pirates piled into two or three cars for the grueling trips to places like Bemidji, trips which required the team to drive several hours, often over gravel roads. Coach Kerrigan always drove his car. Either Erwin Warner or Superintendent Arnold Kittleson drove the second car. Players packed in the cars like sardines.

Space was tight. Darrel Hesby preferred to occupy the middle seat in the back where he could sit with his arms extended to keep from getting sweaty. If it was warm outside, such as it was in the summer when the baseball teams drove to their games, using much the same arrangement, Hesby's middle seat in the back also meant less breeze from the windows to mess up his hair, which was always perfectly parted.

The quiet kids might end up in Coach Kerrigan's car, while the rowdier types piled into Erwin Warner's jalopy. Warner was less proper than Kerrigan, shouting once as they bounced at seventy miles per hour over country intersections, "Wait till we get a decent road, we'll really give 'er hell!"

Sometimes Warner had the players drive. He prodded them to go faster. Erwin had put a notch at seventy miles per hour, it turns out, where the accelerator would catch, and you could relax as if you had cruise control.

After the loss to Grand Rapids, conference games

started and the Halstad Pirates were ready. Their first foe was Fertile. Winners of the district the previous season, Fertile had lost most of their players to graduation, yet they still played a tough defensive game. Unlike the previous year, when Halstad struggled against tough defensive teams with height, the 1951-52 team took Fertile to the cleaners. Halstad's shooting was off, but they poured on the defense. Guard Morrie Holm's exceptional rebounding was a pleasant surprise. If the speedy but diminutive Pirates were going to win, they had to get the ball back. Holm's rebounding and strong athleticism would be a highlight of the team's season, whether or not he scored in double figures.

Another sign of things to come: Don Thompson led the scoring with 14 points in the 44-30 victory of Fertile. Jimmy Akason scored 11, Holm 7, Hesby 5. By the end of the season, seven different players would lead the team in scoring in various games. Opponents could no longer shut Halstad down by focusing defense on one man.

After defeating three lesser conference foes by large scores, Kerrigan loaded up the team in the cars and took them 105 miles to Valley City, North Dakota, for a game against Lisbon, North Dakota. Lisbon featured an athletic center named Gene Gimosh. Halstad easily defeated Lisbon, but during the game Gimosh blocked several of

Halstad center Don Thompson's shots. Thompson was frustrated enough to study the problem and practice backing away from big centers while shooting.

"That really helped the team," said Roger Stole, a Halstad basketball player who graduated the previous year. "Don seems to have learned something from Gimosh." Thompson continued to learn as the season progressed. His contributions to the team increased right to the final game of the season.

According to the Halstad student newspaper, the game in Valley City was beneficial for another reason: It was played on a court with a glass backboard. It was already known around the conference that Hendrum's new gym would be equipped with a glass backboard, and fans wondered how the players would react.

Thanks to its experienced team, led by five-year varsity veterans Jimmy Akason and Darrel Hesby and three others who had started for at least three years, Halstad was the early season favorite to win the conference. Some newspapers even chose Halstad to win their first district title, which was Coach Kerrigan's stated pre-season goal. But one nearby rival made Ray Kerrigan particularly nervous: The neighboring Ada Vikings.

Ada, eighteen miles across the prairie to the east, is

the Norman County seat. In the early 1950s, its population was nearly three times that of Halstad's. The rivalry between the two towns was intense.

"There was no love," said Ada star Dick Nielson, looking back on the time today.

Tickets were scarce for the two games the two teams played one another each year. Indeed, one Halstad fan reserved tickets by phone and drove 250 miles to see the two teams play in Halstad back in 1950.

Ada's basketball team was always tough, thanks to their coach, Dan Ruoff. Ruoff was widely considered the best coach in the district. Fertile lost out in the regional tournament in 1951 after beating Ruoff's Ada team in the district final. Even though Fertile won the game, today a former Fertile player still grumbles, "If we would have had Ruoff as our coach, we could have gone to state."

Ruoff didn't have Ray Kerrigan's bluster or arrogance, but he had a talent for discovering an opponent's weaknesses and exploiting them. Kerrigan knew this, and was never comfortable playing Ada. The more you played the Vikings, the better prepared Ruoff had his teams.

Due to the proximity of the towns, most of the people on the opposite sides of the gym during an Ada vs. Halstad contest knew each other. Rumors still float around of some betting between neighbors near the frontier between the two school districts. Due to the intensity of the rivalry, beating Ada in basketball was probably one of the most important tasks of any Halstad coach. No wonder Kerrigan was nervous.

During the 1951-52 season, the two teams faced off in Halstad on December 17. Ada was off their game in Halstad's gym. The Pirates won easily, 62-41.

After easily defeating Lisbon and old nemesis Waubun, a game in which Dale Serum exploded for 20 points, the Pirates faced Ada again in mid-January of 1952, this time in Ada's gym.

Ada's paper, the *Norman County Index*, previewed the game. "The league leading rampaging Halstad Pirates come for a return game with the Ada Vikings on Saturday evening of this week. Halstad has gone without a defeat thus far and are living up to the advance dope of district favorite. They have a fast, rangy, shifty outfit with years of experience playing together."

Apparently the *Norman County Index* didn't consider Halstad's loss to Grand Rapids an official defeat. The Pirates were indeed undefeated in the conference. The newspaper went on to predict a "battle royal," despite Halstad having an acknowledged edge going in.

"Ada did not play up to their full ability in the game played recently at Halstad and they are out to show their neighbors to the west that this time they are going to make a real battle of it."

The game drew a "tournament-sized crowd." At ten past seven in the evening, the doors on the Ada gym were locked. The building was already crowded far beyond capacity, this before fire codes placed a legal limit on the size of crowds in public buildings.

The expected battle didn't materialize. Although Ada shaved 1 point from the previous spread, the Vikings still lost 60-40. The Ada paper said that, although the Ada team played below par, "There is no question that the speed, aggressiveness, shiftiness, clever ball handling, and floor play of the Pirates has a lot to do with making another team look not so good."

Akason led scorers with 17 points, Bernhagen contributed 14, and Hesby finished with 13.

Aggressiveness. Speed. Clever ball handling—and "shiftiness," whatever that might mean. Halstad was described by its rival town's paper in admiring terms, but with a bite. There was a reason for the subtle digs.

Teams who played Halstad didn't particularly like the Pirates' approach to the game. Their run-and-gun style, first legitimatized only eight years before by tiny Lynd, still grated on some traditionalists. Halstad's coach, Ray Kerrigan, with his wild mop of curly hair and his obvious air of confidence—some say arrogance—rubbed some opponents the wrong way. Hesby's confidence on the floor, along with his uncanny ability to position himself well, might have been the source of the description of the Halstad team as "shifty." Jimmy Akason's baritone commands echoed throughout the entire gymnasium as the team rushed from one end of the floor. His voice became an all-too familiar sound to Halstad opponents and their fans for at least four years.

When fifth-year starter Akason walked onto the court for a game during his senior season, an opponent's cheerleader looked at him incredulously and said, "You mean you're still here?"

What's more, Halstad's play was quite physical for the time. Kerrigan and the team were well aware that they needed to make up in aggressiveness what they lacked in height. Aggressiveness meant fouls. With Halstad's depth and balance, the Pirates weren't afraid to play rough. In fact, Jimmy Akason fouled out more often his senior year than not. Meanwhile, the star player for Thief River Falls, genteel center Roger Williamson, hadn't fouled out all season—that is until Thief River's memorable final game of the year.

So today, when you ask former opponents of Halstad's, gentlemen who are now in their seventies, some of whom later became friends and acquaintances of members of Halstad's 1952 team, what they thought of Halstad's team at the time, they get quiet. Between the hems and haws comes a quiet message: They were cocky, pushy, and we didn't particularly like them.

For the third consecutive season, Kerrigan scheduled the Pirates to travel to Thief River Falls for a regular-season, non-conference game on January 22, 1952. A blizzard intervened. The game was postponed for a week. The make-up date fell during an already busy part of the schedule. By the time their next week was over, the Pirates had played six games in nine days, three of them on the road.

First, the Pirates took on Gary, Minnesota, at home on a Friday night. By the beginning of the second quarter, the game had gotten so out of hand in Halstad's favor that Kerrigan pulled the five starters and put in the reserves. At half-time, Kerrigan had the Starting Five dress in street clothes. The subs didn't slow down. The final score was 103-32.

Despite the lopsided score, the Gary game was, according to the Halstad paper, "one of the most thrilling games of the year." The second stringers, eager to prove themselves, "gave one of the finest exhibitions of passing and shooting that we have seen all season."

When others saw the score, they accused Kerrigan of pouring it on. They didn't seem to notice the futile measures he had taken to avoid that perception. And certainly, Kerrigan wasn't of a mind to tell the subs to ease up on the Gary team when they were finally allowed to get on the floor in an A squad game.

The next evening, Saturday night, Halstad defeated Twin Valley in a conference game 68-48. The boys took Sunday off, went to school Monday, and practiced Monday night. After school Tuesday night, the team piled in the cars for the long trip north to Thief River Falls.

Although they always looked forward to playing on the regulation-sized floor in Thief River, on this night the team was flat. Their shots were off. Thief River Falls got along fine without its star center, Roger Williamson, who played no more than a few minutes in the second half due to a bout of the flu. But the remaining Prowlers had height. They had a promising sophomore named Art Johnson, a ball handler named Dick Bjorkman, and a great all-around athlete in Gary Anderson. They kept the ball away from Halstad, stifled the Pirate running game, and won 45-42. After a stunning victory over Thief River Falls two years before, Halstad had lost two straight close games in the Brick House in Thief River.

After putting in the next day at school, the Pirates traveled 110 miles in the opposite direction from Thief River in the gymnasium at Moorhead State Teachers College. Kerrigan had them playing for a March of Dimes benefit. He hadn't put the game on the schedule until mid-January. He hadn't anticipated that the Thief River Falls postponement would force the Pirates to play on two consecutive school nights far from home. In his eagerness to find opponents, Kerrigan had run his team to a frazzle.

At the Moorhead State gym, Halstad was to play Comstock, Minnesota, a town of less than two hundred people south of Moorhead. Comstock was a balanced team as well, and the team had a good coach, George Farr. Farr, who later became chairman of Minnesota's Democratic Farmer-Labor Party, had taken the unusual step of traveling to see Halstad play Twin Valley the week before. Advance scouting of opponents was unheard of at the time, but Farr used it to his advantage. The Comstock team beat a tired and flat Halstad bunch by a score of 49-42. It was an upset of the "vaunted Halstad team," according to the *Fargo Forum*, although a sports columnist wrote, "Those two losses could be the making of their tournament team." He anticipated that Halstad would recover in a hurry.

In the crowd that night were ballplayers from all around the area, some who had played in other games for the same polio benefit. They took the opportunity to heckle the famous Jimmy Akason from the stands and rub in the defeat. When Akason attended college the next year, the hecklers would become some of his best friends.

Ray Kerrigan realized that the high-stepping Pirates' two defeats were due in part to spending two consecutive nights on the road and facing two strong, non-conference opponents. Despite the difficult circumstances, Ray Kerrigan was not happy. He and assistant Larry Macleod sat down and plotted strategy. The next night's practice featured extra work and a couple of new twists.

Kerrigan's practices: They are remembered most for what they were not. When the bell rang ending classes for the day, the boys would race to the locker room to get dressed for practice—and to get their hands on the best of the mostly ragged practice basketballs. They shot around on the floor while Kerrigan went down to the boiler room to have a cigarette or two—or three—with the janitors. Eventually, often forty-five minutes after school ended, Kerrigan would enter the gym, climb to the top of the bleachers, loosen his tie, pull out a whistle, and preside over a forty-five minute scrimmage. After the scrimmage, the players might jump some rope before Kerrigan would hand them their vitamin pill and send them to the showers. No running laps. No drills. No rehearsal of pre-planned plays.

What planned moves the team employed on the court had been developed by the boys themselves over years of playing together. Their plays were intuitive rather than designed play based on actual Xs and Os. Akason directed the action on the floor, but he never held up one, two, or three fingers as a signal. He barked, and the others knew where to go. By the 1952 season, the Starting Five had played together so long that they knew exactly where each other would be.

Kerrigan's approach to practice might have seemed lax. However, the boys were anything but laid back during practice. They competed with each other. Aside from buddies Jimmy Akason and Darrel Hesby, they weren't particularly close off the court.

"We sometimes nearly broke into fisticuffs," Dale

Serum remembers fifty-five years later. "But then Jim would shape us up."

"He was our leader," Serum added offhandedly, as if he was merely reasserting the obvious.

"You didn't want to be left out," said Darrel Hesby. "If somebody else succeeded, you wanted to do well, too."

The competition between the players, kept in reasonable check by Akason and Kerrigan, rather than cause disruption, seemed to improve the players.

How did Jimmy Akason handle his role as the unquestioned leader of the Halstad Pirates? Was he resented? Was he cocky? Were the others jealous of his talent, his regional fame, his dominating presence on the court and off?

The questions drew a long pause from a former teammate.

"To us," said the player, who graduated before Jimmy Akason and lost considerable playing time to the younger Akason over the years, "Jimmy Akason was ten feet tall."

Nobody recalls Akason lording his status over the rest. Perhaps his teammates respected him because they knew that while Jim's father Martin was alive, Jim faced relentless grilling about his performance. Perhaps they respected Jim because after Martin passed away just before the 1951-52 school year, they knew that things were tough in the Akason household. Perhaps they respected Jimmy Akason simply because he carried himself like he was ten feet tall.

Yes, Akason and Hesby could be ball hogs earlier in their careers. Yes, Kerrigan had to cool the pair's jets by sitting them down their junior year against Hillsboro. But there was never any question who the star of the 1952 team was, no matter how many others might on some given night lead the scoring: It was Jimmy Akason.

Akason and Hesby were close friends, but the rest of the team didn't spend much time together off the court— even though there were only twenty-six students in the class of 1952. Don Thompson was desperately in love with his sweetheart Jane, with whom he spent every spare moment. Because of his boyhood arm injury, Thompson didn't play baseball in the summers with the other guys. If Don Thompson wasn't with Jane, he was out trying to hustle up some money by working. In fact, while Dale Serum spent summers as the catcher for the town team, Don Thompson, already determined to make a good living, went to work for Serum's father Orlando building houses.

Morrie Holm lived five miles from town. Like most farm boys, he had to work when he wasn't playing ball. He spent no time hanging around town. Holm spent more time with neighbor Marlyn Aanenson, an equally shy farm boy and a reserve on the basketball team, than he spent with others of the Starting Five. Dale Serum sometimes joined up with Jim and Darrel to drive to Shelly to chase girls. But Serum was a quiet, self-sufficient sort, not one to chum around. Serum did spend more time with new arrival Chuck Bernhagen than anybody, but that was mostly because Serum worked for Erwin Warner, Bernhagen's uncle. Bernhagen wasn't in Halstad long, and nobody seems to have known him that well at all.

On the court, however, the team functioned as a unit. Selfish play earned time on the bench. Kerrigan had led a bomber crew on dozens of dangerous missions only eight years before. He knew better than most that everybody had to row in the one direction for the team to win.

Akason and Thompson developed a rapport on the floor despite barely knowing each other off it. Akason enjoyed working with Thompson because, unlike some centers he would eventually play with in college ball, "When you threw the ball to Don, you knew you might get it back."

They developed moves which, when the two got together fifty-five years later to reminisce, they swore they could still repeat. Some big centers can't catch the ball. Thompson's soft hands earned him the respect of those whose job it was to get the ball to him.

By the time they were seniors, the Starting Five plus Bernhagen were well-developed athletes with a strong sense of their own abilities. Although Akason was the leader, he was aware that he no longer was hands-down the best athlete on the floor. Today, Hesby and Akason talk of their successful sophomore season with special nostalgia. Both wave off their personal statistics during their final 1952 season as merely average, at least given their previous performance. Still, they are proudest of the team effort of 1952.

"By our senior year, the others had developed and were just plain good," Akason says today. "I am not sure I ever told them that," he adds with characteristic worry, for if Martin Akason taught Jimmy one thing, it was to be a gentleman.

Akason needn't worry. Serum, Holm, Thompson and Bernhagen knew very well that they were good. When the Starting Five minus Bernhagen (who passed away in the 1970s) gathered in Cora Stennes' living room fifty-three years later to relive the 1952 season, their confidence permeated the room.

"You saw them sitting there," Clarence Stennes said after the meeting. "They're still..." He meant to say "cocky," but couldn't quite get it out. The word was a too harsh for what he meant.

Yet, even assuming the Starting Five's demeanor has mellowed some in the past fifty-three years, enough pride remained in their bearing in 2005 to infer that in 1952 the Starting Five hadn't been shy and retiring.

Who instilled that confidence? Only Jimmy Akason and Darrel Hesby may have come by it naturally. They were the town kids. Kids about town are generally pretty comfortable with their position in the world.

As for the rest, one can only assume that the sheer energy, force of personality, and bubbling ebullience of Ray Kerrigan, who coached most of the boys in three sports for at least three years, rubbed off on young men who otherwise might have gone through life as quiet and self-effacing as their own fathers and mothers.

As the season wore on through the dark winter months, March Madness approached. Each winter, the superintendents of the schools in District 30, and sometimes the coaches, would meet to determine the format.

Every year they had to reinvent the wheel. Controversy raged over whether the teams should be seeded so the team with the best record would play the team with the worst record in the first round. The poorer teams lobbied to have the pairings drawn from a hat. The better teams wanted to be seeded. Generally, the better teams won the day, but not until several secret ballots decided the question.

The next decision: Where would the games be held? Of course, the school with the biggest gym was the logical choice. But what if that school, which in Halstad's district was Fertile, was competitive? Wouldn't it be unfair to have the games on their home court?

In 1952, it took two meetings to organize the tournament for Halstad's subdistrict. Coaches and superintendents attended both. There was no love lost between the school's representatives as the meetings stretched into the evening with proposal after proposal and ballot after ballot.

When the men finally decided, they released the results to the newspapers. Most of the local rags ran the story on the front page, under a bigger headline than any of the previous basketball games of that year. Fans wanted to know: Where were the tournament games going to be?

Will we be able to get tickets? Who will we play first? Even the referees for each game were announced weeks in advance.

All tickets were reserved. Adult tickets were $1, student tickets 50 cents. You could purchase a few advance tickets from the superintendent's office of each competing school. For the remaining seats, fans had to stand in line at the tournament site, sometimes for hours. One Halstad fan remembers today standing in line for three hours to get a ticket for a crucial game. She was nine months pregnant at the time.

In 1952, the subdistrict games would be played in two locations. Hendrum's new gym was ready, so half the games would be held there, with Hendrum's superintendent promising to clear the football field of snow to provide parking under lights. The rest of the games would be held in Fertile, which had the biggest gym in the subdistrict at the time. Incredibly, consolation games would decide every position from third through eighth.

The high school basketball tournaments were an extended affair for one reason: Ticket revenues. Tournament planners knew they could draw a good crowd for a game to decide the seventh place finisher in the subdistrict, so they put it on the schedule. In the early 1950s, high school basketball was popular enough for even the most inconsequential game to draw a crowd.

Judging from the results of the regular season, Halstad had no real competition in the sub-district tournament. Yet, Kerrigan was wary. His team had faltered in the tournaments two years in a row, and Halstad's sub-district included Dan Ruoff's Ada Vikings, who Kerrigan feared. This was Kerrigan's best team yet, but only one of his previous teams, all of them also very promising, had advanced as far as the district tournaments.

Then illness struck. Darrel Hesby was the first to get sick. He developed a terrific sore throat. Red streaks developed on his skin. He went to the doctor and was diagnosed with scarletina, otherwise known as scarlet fever. A penicillin shot improved matters greatly, but not before Hesby lost about a week of practice and playing time. He would be on shaky legs for some time. Before the ordeal was over, he lost fifteen pounds—and he had no surplus to begin with.

Then Don Thompson got the flu. Kerrigan visited the Thompson household to inform him that for the first round of subdistricts against Borup, the mainstay center was to stay in bed. Thompson's replacement, Frankie Steenerson, had a fine game and marched right into Don

Thompson's house afterwards to tell him about it, grinning from ear to ear. Thompson dressed for the next game against Hendrum, but when he got in the game, he could tell it wasn't going to work, so Kerrigan sat him down.

Valuable reserve Marlyn "Lefty" Aanenson also came down with scarlet fever and was out for a week.

Finally, Jim Akason developed a cough. Kerrigan insisted he go to the doctor. Because Halstad's physician, Dr. Erickson, was himself sick, Akason traveled to Ada to see Dr. Boyington and was diagnosed with measles.

Akason never broke out, but word of his illness spread across the prairie like a rash. The rumor no doubt sent the hearts of opposing fans aflutter, Ada fans in particular. These were not times when you politely wished prospective opponents good health, especially if they were the high-stepping Halstad Pirates.

When Jim Akason, by then almost recovered, walked into the locker room in Fertile to get dressed for the first game of the sub-district tournaments, the tournament manager, Fertile's superintendent E. M. Knalson, pointed at him and said, "Who said you could play?"

Akason was ready for the question. He had requested a note from Dr. Boyington that cleared him to compete. The superintendent was skeptical, but consented. Once

Knalson granted Akason permission to play, Kerrigan brushed it all off and said, "We aren't going to play him anyway."

Such was the depth of Halstad's bench. The Pirates made it through the first rounds of the subdistrict tournaments with their three top players each missing entire games due to illness.

After Halstad easily defeated Borup and Hendrum, the sub-district final pitted Pirates against archrival Ada. Just as Kerrigan feared, Ada's coach Ruoff had his boys ready. The two regular season losses of 20 points each to Halstad were forgotten. Ada came out running at the Fertile gym. Ada had a large cheering section, and they had a plan.

For three quarters, the Ada Vikings outran the Pirates. The Vikings' big cheering section was "given a tremendous thrill as they saw their favorites not only play those fast-stepping Pirates on even terms, but actually having a little the better of the argument through most of this time." For those three quarters, "It was as beautiful a championship game as you could wish to see anywhere," according to the Halstad paper. Ada led for three quarters, once by as much as 9 points, assisted by 25 points from their star, Dick Nielson. At the end of the third quarter, the score was tied 49-49. Kerrigan's worst fears had been realized. In the huddle at end of the third quarter, he gave the team the third degree.

Then Ada ran out of gas. Halstad outscored the Vikings 15-3 in the last quarter and took the game 64-52. Halstad had played run-and-gun all season. They were used to the pace. Ada's daring plan to out-run the Pirates didn't take into account that their legs hadn't run like that for an entire game all year.

Although winning the subdistricts was a thrill for Halstad, the championship game was rendered less meaningful due to the rules of the time which allowed the top two teams—both Ada and Halstad—to advance to the eight-team district tournament. To Ray Kerrigan's chagrin, the Halstad Pirates weren't done with Dan Ruoff's boys yet.

On to the district tourney. The 1952 Minnesota District 30 tournament was held in Fosston's double-decker gym. Ada and Halstad were the co-favorites, despite Halstad's three previous defeats of the Vikings.

Using ample reserves, Ray Kerrigan's boys easily disposed of McIntosh in the first round. The second round pitted Halstad against the always pesky Waubun Bombers. Although they trailed at the half, and led by only 2 points after three periods, Halstad's superior depth wore down Waubun boys in the fourth quarter, and Halstad pulled away with a 50-41 victory.

Meanwhile, Ada charged past Fosston and Bagley to set up the predicted rematch with the Halstad Pirates for the district title. Prognosticators, citing Ada coach Dan Ruoff's expertise and the Vikings' impressive showing in the first two games of the tournament, figured the game was a toss-up.

Although Ada led by 1 point after the first quarter, Halstad's depth kicked in. Midway through the fourth quarter, Halstad held a lead of 5 points and began to stall. By the end, the Ada Vikings managed to shave points off their previous margin of defeat to Halstad, but they lost by a score of 50-41. Don Thompson led Halstad's scoring with 15 points. Akason and Bernhagen followed with 14 and 10 points, respectively.

Ray Kerrigan had his district title. It was Halstad's first. He had defeated the archrival Ada Vikings and their talented coach Ruoff four times in one season.

Ruoff's reputation as a coach among his peers was untarnished by the losses to the deeper, faster Halstad Pirates. Nevertheless, losing four times to the rivals across the prairie wasn't the town of Ada's idea of a successful season. When the next season rolled around, Dan Ruoff was no longer the Vikings' coach.

The *Norman County Index* was gracious in defeat of their hometown team. "It was a pleasing victory for Halstad," the *Index* wrote, citing the Pirates' previous three years of "knocking at the door with this group of rather brilliant players" without winning a title. Halstad's undefeated conference record and previous defeats of Ada made "it [seem] right that they should win the coveted crown."

As Ada star Dick Nielson said fifty-five years later, there was no love between the Halstad Pirates and the Ada Vikings—and no love between the people of the two towns, for that matter. But in 1952, the Ada people buried the hatchet, at least for a month's time, and got behind the exceptional basketball team from their neighboring town fifteen miles across the wheat fields.

As the *Index* noted, the players for Halstad were largely the same as the previous years' teams. However, the Pirate bunch that was on the floor during the tournaments in 1952 was more experienced, more developed, and more balanced. Jimmy Akason, still on shaky legs from the measles, had for most of the tournament passed the scoring torch to Dale Serum. It was Serum and Chuck

Bernhagen who carried the Halstad Pirates through the games when Halstad's more famous stars were ailing or well-defended. Although Serum wasn't known as a shooter, when he got on a roll, he could take over a game and drive the ball to the basket with the best of them.

Regionals—here we come. Kerrigan had done no planning for the four-team regional tournament. He had sent no scouts to view the District 32 final which would produce Halstad's first round opponent. The champion of District 32, Karlstad, had gone through the season with twenty-two wins and no defeats, but their schedule had included only teams from within their district. Prognosticators, including Thief River Falls sports writing legend Huck Olson, chose Halstad to win the first round in a walk.

In the other first-round game, Thief River Falls played the team from the Red Lake Indian Reservation. Basketball was popular on the reservation, and the Red Lake team occasionally made its mark against the area's bigger teams. In district play, the Red Lakers had shocked perennial region champion Bemidji, a team that was, admittedly, having a rebuilding year under coach Bun Fortier. Sportswriter Huck Olson had traveled to Bemidji to see the district final, and he came away astonished by the Red Lake team's inspired play.

Even so, nobody gave Red Lake a chance. The newspapers disregarded them as "the Indian entry" into the tournament. In a preview of the tournament, the *Fargo Forum* wrote that the winner of the Karlstad vs. Halstad game would have to face the Thief River Falls Prowlers, even though the game between Thief River and Red Lake had not yet been played.

The prognosticators were correct. Thief River disposed of Red Lake easily. And Halstad defeated Karlstad without a problem. Dale Serum again was the star, leading the scoring with 16 points. Bernhagen scored 13, Akason 12. Marlyn Aanenson again played a role, scoring 10 points. Kerrigan used his entire bench, even working his way down to the last player, popular "Squirt" George Allen Johnson, a senior whose playing time throughout the year had been extremely limited.

The victories by Halstad on Wednesday night and Thief River Falls on Thursday night set up a Saturday evening regional final between the region's two best teams. Tickets for the game were scarce despite the 2,100 seats in the Brick House at Lincoln School in Thief River Falls. Fans had best be friends with the superintendent of schools or be willing to stand in line for hours in the cold to get in.

Kerrigan had to be happy with his position going in. Having survived illnesses to some of his best players without losing in tournament play, Kerrigan's team was now more experienced and even more well-rounded. In the qualifying games, reserves had played important roles. Even Franklin Steenerson, who had played only a few minutes during the season, led the scoring in a tournament game when Thompson had the flu. Dale Serum was coming into his own. Marlyn Aanenson showed cool under fire. Akason and Hesby were back at full strength. Don Thompson, long over his bout with the flu, was looking solid. Chuck Bernhagen had made vital contributions when the others were down. Morrie Holm, although he hadn't been scoring much during the tournaments, was an ace rebounder, a good dribbler, and a physical player. Darrel Hesby still had the good shot that had gotten him on the floor as a freshman. Going into the game of their lives against Thief River Falls, the Halstad Pirates were firing on all cylinders.

Chapter 8

The Biggest Game of the Year

Little Clarence Stennes' legs dangled from the chair in Superintendent Arnold Kittleson's office at the Halstad school. His father, Alvin Stennes, sat next to him. They were there to pick up their tickets for the game that night, and Kittleson had called them in to his office for a visit. Tickets were scarce. Each town was allotted a block, and it was up to the superintendent of each school to distribute them fairly.

Kittleson turned to Clarence. "So, what do you think?" he asked. "Do we stand a chance?"

Clarence soberly explained that Thief River Falls had the height advantage and that might be too much, but that he thought Halstad could pull it out.

Things had happened so fast. One week before, Halstad had won the district title. Then they beat Karlstad. Now the Pirates were a tantalizing one game away from becoming a part of the biggest event on the Minnesota sports calendar. The heroes Clarence had followed since he had been aware of the world around him stood on the verge of unimaginable glory. Clarence didn't dare get his hopes too high, but not so deep down, he knew how close his Pirates were.

It wasn't only Clarence. The entire town of Halstad pulsed with adrenaline. The stoic Norwegians, for whom the outward expression of joy or sorrow was generally unfamiliar, could barely contain themselves. What if the Pirates actually won? A state tournament trip was so close, but still so improbable. Nobody dared talk seriously about it.

Jeanette Enger of Halstad was a sophomore at Concordia College in Moorhead. She called home. Could her dad get some tickets for the game? He would try. Jeanette planned to drive back to Halstad for the weekend, just in case.

The region final would be played at the Brick House in Thief River Falls. For the Prowlers, it would be a home game. Organizers generally tried to schedule region tournaments at neutral sites, usually at the fieldhouse at an area university. However, in 1952 the Brick House was the biggest venue available and the logical choice for the final.

Not that the Halstad Pirates cared. In fact, they looked forward to playing on the regulation floor in the Brick House. The large court suited Halstad's running game well. The team had played in the gym three times in the past three years, thanks to Erwin Warner's connection to his first cousin, Thief River Falls coach Bob Nick. One of the team's most important victories had come there two years before. Darrel Hesby, Jim Akason, Don Thompson, and Lefty Aanenson had played on the team when Halstad shocked Thief River Falls in late 1948. The victory awakened Halstad to the potential of its then-young team, and now, a long three years later, that potential finally had been realized.

But the Thief River Falls team also had been young in 1949. By 1952, they had a core group of five players who had grown up together. All town boys who lived a few blocks apart, they had played together in their neighborhood since they were children. In fact, several of them drove to school together every day in an old Model A.

The Prowlers' star was Roger Williamson, their six-foot-five-inch center. He usually scored half the team's points. But he was surrounded by friends. Dick Bjorkman was a fancy ball-handler with a good move to the basket and a slick jump shot. Gary Anderson, a great all-around athlete and football star also played. Big Stan Rosengren, Charles "Bobo" Dicken, and Don Johnson rounded out the starters. Johnson's 1952 season ended before it started with a hernia, but the rest of the group was expected to go places, and had been expected to do so for quite some time.

Going places for the Thief River Falls Prowlers meant something different than it did for the humble Halstad Pirates. The Prowlers had not only gone to the state tournament five times, but they won state titles in 1932 and 1937. They had a basketball tradition. The town had been watching this group develop and grow over four years, and they expected their boys to return the Prowlers to past glory.

To add to expectations, the Prowlers boasted a promising newcomer in 1951. When the Thief River Falls school hired a new industrial arts teacher named Art Johnson, he brought with him his son Art "Sonny" Johnson, Jr. The elder Johnson was a crusty sort, prone to revolting his students with graphic descriptions of sliced-off fingers and mangled limbs in an attempt to get them to take seriously the machinery they worked on in industrial arts class. And he loved basketball—so much so that he showed up for every practice to watch his son, Art Jr., who was six-foot-four and loaded with talent.

Like his father, Art Jr. wasn't overly concerned about winning friends and influencing people. He kept to himself. When he spoke, he could be gruff. The others on the team didn't take kindly to Art Jr. elbowing his way on to the team, and he didn't much care.

It didn't help that Bob Nick had become friends with the elder Johnson. Bob Nick was the sort of coach who chose his starting five and stuck with them. When Art Johnson, Jr. broke the starting five, he displaced the other four players' friend, Charles "Bobo" Dicken. The rest of the team was offended by Johnson's ascension to the starting lineup as a mere sophomore—particularly when it displaced a senior who was their buddy, and particularly when cranky Art Johnson Sr. was at every practice looking over Coach Bob Nick's shoulder.

Like Ray Kerrigan, Bob Nick lacked much knowledge of basketball's nuts and bolts. In fact, when asked about Bob Nick as a basketball coach, most Thief River Falls old timers respond that he made a very good football coach.

"You had to pick up the technical stuff on your own," said a former player. "It just wasn't there."

What strategy Nick did employ was sometimes questioned by his team. Their discontent wasn't limited to Art Johnson's appearance in their midst as a sophomore. Nick's tendency to stick with five players and five players only made the reserves feel out of the loop. And despite having a tall team for the time, Bob Nick wanted his boys to play run-and-gun when the wiser option might have been to control the ball and slow things down.

Unlike the fiery, hot-headed Ray Kerrigan, Bob Nick was downright bland. A nice guy by everybody's admission, he was out of place attempting to light a fire under a team. Nick was prim. He was serious. He was a strict disciplinarian. And he hadn't connected with his Thief River Prowlers in the way the charismatic Ray Kerrigan had connected with his Halstad Pirates.

But never mind the coaches. The game is played on the floor, and the way basketball was played at the time gave the players great leeway to free lance as they saw fit. Both the Halstad and Thief River Falls teams had played together for years. They were used to their teammates. Thief River Falls had an enormous height advantage, and they had a big center in Roger Williamson who could pivot either way and who tended not to miss the basket from up close. Don Thompson would have his hands full.

The townspeople of Thief River Falls didn't imagine that Halstad would stand in the way of their returning to their rightful perch in the state's final eight. Their team had beaten Halstad during the regular season even with Roger Williamson out with the flu. How much bigger a margin of victory would be theirs with the mighty Williamson at full strength!

Thief River Falls had been the favorite in Region 8 from the beginning of the season. Although they lost five regular season games, those losses were to opponents from large schools outside the region. Included were two losses to the Grand Forks Central Redskins, who were led by senior Lute Olson and went on to win the North Dakota state title. (Of course, Lute Olson went far beyond his early North Dakota victories to become a preeminent figure on the collegiate basketball landscape, most recently at the University of Arizona where he has guided his teams to 19 consecutive 20-win seasons and is one of only three coaches in NCAA history to record 28 or more 20-win seasons.) Thief River Falls also lost to a strong Moorhead team and in a game on the court in Detroit Lakes in which the hometown scorekeeper stopped the clock for at least twenty seconds, an interlude which allowed the Lakers to score twice and win.

Early in the season, fans and local newspapermen worried that Bob Nick's squad wouldn't be able to handle a fast-break offense. However, when the Prowlers defeated traditional Region 8 power Bemidji, coached by the legendary Bun Fortier, who always pressed on defense and ran hard on offense, those concerns were laid to rest.

Thief River fans also worried early in the season that the Prowlers were too dependent upon their star, Roger

Williamson. What if he were well-defended? Those worries were put to the test when a good East Grand Forks team tried to foil the Prowlers by collapsing three players around Williamson. The other four Prowlers stepped into the void. Thief River built a 18-2 lead without a single basket from their big man. After the East Grand Forks game, it was clear that the Prowlers were not a one-man show.

Thief River Falls Lincoln High School was ten times the size of Halstad's school, and unlike Halstad, the school was big enough to carry two winter sports, basketball and hockey. During the 1950s, hockey was on the rise. The two sports divided the talent pool. One of the greatest athletes in Minnesota history, Thief River's Jack Erickson, chose hockey over basketball. If he had gone the other way, the Prowlers would have had an even more formidable basketball team. As it was, basketball was still popular in the town, owing to the spectacular success of the Prowlers in the 1930s.

Early in 1952 the Prowler pucksters had gone to the state tournament. They were regarded as one of the best hockey teams Thief River had put on the ice up to that time. However, when the hockey team made an early exit from the state tourney, it was left to the town's pumpkin pushers to bring the town the athletic glory it felt it deserved.

Halstad and Thief River Falls are both towns in north-western Minnesota populated primarily by Norwegian immigrants. The similarities end there. A logging town in its early days, at least until the trees ran out, Thief River Falls had a rough-and-tumble history. Prostitution was once well-entrenched on the western edge of town. When the call girls came downtown to shop, the more reputable residents scurried away with their young daughters lest their young ones see the elaborate finery of the girls of the evening and get entrepreneurial ideas of their own.

The Red Lake Indian reservation, which begins a few miles east of Thief River, is the only piece of land within the United States borders to never have been ceded to the United States government. It, too, retained an edge of wildness. Teepees and Indians on horseback were common sights just east of Thief River well into the 1920s. Adding to the mystery of the frontier east of Thief River is the great Beltrami forest, an impenetrable tract of millions of acres of swamp, bog and woods. Hunters have been known to disappear in this area never to be found, and escaped convicts have hidden out there for decades—at least if one believes local lore.

The 1950s were a particularly rough time in the Thief River Falls school. Local gangs brought in drugs, mostly—but not exclusively—marijuana. One can find "drug seminars" promoted in the local paper as early as 1951. Rumbles between Thief River thugs and boys from Crookston and other neighboring towns took place in the cemetery, or outside the gym after a ball game. At least two high school principals in quick succession just couldn't handle the duck-tailed rowdies. Eventually a principal was hired who was physically capable of throwing the toughs out the front door and down the front steps, and he didn't hesitate to do so.

Quite a contrast to placid little Halstad. Not that life was completely innocent farther out on the prairie in a town of 500, but the kids who grew up in Halstad during the early 1950s were, by Thief River Falls standards, quite sheltered. Principal Ray Kerrigan never had to throw anybody out the front door of the school—although he, too, wouldn't have hesitated.

Despite the eighty miles between the two towns, there were connections between Halstad and Thief River Falls. Prowler coach Bob Nick had worked on his cousin Erwin Warner's farm near Halstad during the previous summer. Nick's relation to Warner had resulted in Thief River putting Halstad on its schedule for the three previous years. In addition, Palmer Anderson, the father of Thief River Falls' guard Gary Anderson, had been raised in the Halstad area. Palmer's brother Arnie Anderson still lived in Halstad.

The Anderson brothers had done well in the road construction business, first together and then separately. They were hale and hardy good old boys who liked their whiskey, and it was no surprise to anybody that they put money down on the game between their two home teams. What was shocking was the amount: A $1,000 bet at the time was more than it took to buy the fanciest brand new car on the market. The bet was kept quiet lest the Anderson brothers' formidable wives catch wind of it, in which case there would have been hell to pay on both ends. It is also likely that Gary Anderson had no idea that his father had money riding on the game. While the big bet was in character, it also would not have been like old man Anderson to put that kind of pressure on his son.

Ray Kerrigan's pre-season goal was to win a district title. With that accomplished, any additional victories were simply a bonus. He had known nothing about the Karlstad team, yet Halstad cruised to an easy victory. He knew much more about the Thief River team, and he used the three days between the two games to plot strategy with his advisors, most notably his assistant, Larry

Macleod, and his friend, Erwin Warner.

With their input, Kerrigan decided to harass Roger Williamson all night, even if it meant getting Halstad players into early foul trouble. Because Kerrigan had seven athletes of roughly equal ability, he would rotate defenders on Williamson to avoid any one player's racking up too many fouls. Kerrigan was well aware that he had more experienced and able horses in his stable than did Thief River Falls coach Bob Nick, and he intended to use Halstad's superior depth to his advantage.

Meanwhile, Bob Nick would go with the same starting five which had gotten him through the season. Although the town of Thief River expected an easy victory over Halstad, Nick and his players were under no illusions. They had played Halstad three times in the previous three years, winning twice, but once in overtime and the other time by only 1 point. Thief River Falls sports writer Huck Olson sounded a note of caution in his pre-tournament analysis, saying that the Prowlers would have to "step it up a bit" if they expected a victory over Halstad. Olson's warning was ignored by Thief River Falls fans. This was their year. Olson was just trying not to jinx his town's team with overconfident statements which could be used to motivate the underdog opponent.

Pressure for tickets to the region final at the Brick House was intense. Former Halstad residents called from as far away as Minneapolis. They wanted to drive the 325 miles to Thief River for the game. Superintendent Arnold Kittleson did little else in the days before the Thief River game but attempt to distribute Halstad's allotment fairly. Although the Brick House in Thief River Falls could hold 2,100 fans, those tickets were distributed to schools throughout the region, as well as to Halstad, by school size. On that score, Halstad came out on the short end. Not everybody who wanted to attend the game would be able to get in.

Jeanette Enger of Halstad drove home from Concordia College to find that her father had only been able to land one ticket. The two decided they both would make the drive to Thief River Falls. Old man Enger would use the ticket in the first half while daughter Jeanette sat in the car listening to the game on the radio. In the second half they would swap. The temperature was in the twenties. No doubt the engine idled in the Enger car, and one assumes a window was cracked to avoid carbon monoxide poisoning.

The Brick House, as the gym in the Lincoln High School in Thief River Falls was known, was built by the WPA during the Great Depression. It was the grandest gym in northwestern Minnesota. Its Quonset-style, arched steel rafters soared over the regulation-sized basketball floor, but in the opposite direction one might expect. The roofline ran parallel to and overhead the half-court line and extended far behind each sideline, allowing for two tiers of deep bleachers on each side. Meanwhile, the brick side walls squeezed the court on each either end, leaving players barely three feet in which to inbound the ball after an opponent's basket. On the west side of the gym, high above the basket, was a balcony with seats with a restricted view of the floor. Many Halstad fans ended up in that balcony—probably not by coincidence.

Although the region final would be played on Thief River's home floor, other schools in the region brought their contingents as well. It is possible that Thief River Falls fans were in the minority in their own gym. Because Thief River was the overwhelming favorite and because there wasn't much love lost between the small towns in the region and their larger neighbor, the crowd's sympathies were at least evenly divided between the Pirates and the Prowlers.

A player on the Climax High School team eliminated by the Prowlers in the district tournament attended the game. He pulled for Halstad, violating the tradition that you pulled for the team which knocked you out of the tournaments. He was not alone. Why?

"Those guys were so goddamned cocky," he says today, referring to the Prowlers with a shake of his head.

Halstad was an unlikely region finalist. The Pirates hailed from one of the smallest schools in the region. When the Pirates arrived at the region final, it alerted basketball watchers throughout the state. Even the *Minneapolis Tribune* covered the region final, as did several radio stations. The press of the time was always on the lookout for an underdog and a potential state tournament "darling." By the region final, the state media hounds had found one in Halstad.

The Thief River Falls band, which played at the game, had as its director a man named Bob Harmon. Harmon was a sports nut. So much so, in fact, that he preferred studying sports to directing the band. Harmon took pride in picking winners. As the region tournaments approached, he not only picked Thief River Falls to win in Region 8, but he predicted the winners of the other seven regions in Minnesota before the four-team tournaments even began.

Although the Pirates had all of their players back from illness, the newspapers pondered whether Akason would be at full strength, whether Hesby had his legs back after his bout with scarletina, and whether Aanenson would be able to help off the bench. In fact, Akason was still suffering from a cough and wasn't completely himself.

As the teams warmed up on the Brick House floor, Kerrigan still wasn't sure who he would start at guard. Dale Serum had led the scoring in the game against Karlstad, but that didn't mean he'd have two good games in a row. Kerrigan liked to mix things up, rotating the starting guard position between Serum, Hesby, and Bernhagen, a formula which had worked well all season. But as the buzzer rang, ending the warm-ups and signaling that the game was about to start, Kerrigan made up his mind. Tonight, it would be Serum. Hesby would begin the game on the bench, but would get in the game as soon as the others started to rack up their expected quota of fouls.

A good decision it was. Serum was on fire. He scored Halstad's first five baskets, and the Pirates quickly opened up a 13-3 lead.

Little Clarence Stennes, attending the first basketball game of his life outside of the Halstad gym, jumped out of his seat in the back row of the bleachers with every turn of the game. So far, so good. The Halstad fans were giddy. Their boys were on tonight. They might even pull off the impossible.

The game was rough, as Kerrigan and his advisors had planned. Halstad's attempts to corral Roger Williamson worked in the first period. The Thief River team couldn't get the ball in to their big man and lost the ball many times trying. At the end of the first quarter, Halstad led by a 19-11 score.

In the second period, Coach Bob Nick opened up the Thief River offense. Guards Dick Bjorkman and Gary Anderson pumped in some outside shots. Halstad's attempts to cover the two outside shooters allowed Thief River to get the ball in to Williamson, who scored 8 points in the second quarter. But Halstad matched the Prowlers almost basket-for-basket, heading into the locker room at half-time with a 30-23 lead, only 1 point less than their lead had been at the end of the first quarter.

Kerrigan had to be satisfied, although he certainly didn't let on in the locker room that things were going fine. That wasn't his style. Kerrigan delivered his best, half-time, motivational speeches after the Pirates put in a sub-par first half. If Halstad trailed at the half, you could bet they'd come out guns ablaze in the third quarter. But holding a 7 point lead over Thief River Falls in the region final, as preferable as it was to being 7 points down, was an awkward position. To make matters worse, the Pirates were in foul trouble—thanks to Kerrigan's aggressive strategy of sending player after player in to rough up Roger Williamson. Kerrigan couldn't fault his players. They had done just what he had told them to, even though Williamson had scored all but 7 of Thief River's first-half points. Now, the Pirates were at risk of losing Akason, Thompson, and Holm to fouls. Each had three. They would have to lay back a bit in the third quarter.

Meanwhile, trouble for Halstad brewed in the Thief River Falls locker room. For once, Bob Nick's bland personality and flat demeanor worked to his team's advantage. He didn't panic. The players realized on their own that their season hung in the balance. They were on the verge of losing to a bunch of hicks from a no-count town, and on their home court to boot. That was unacceptable. What divisions there were on the team evaporated as the gravity of the situation sank in. If they didn't get their act together, the exhalted Prowlers wouldn't even get the chance to go to state, much less reclaim the state title for Thief River Falls.

After the half, the Prowlers came out firing on all cylinders. Big Roger Williamson continued his torrid offensive show, shooting hooks, fade aways, and pivot shots. Stan Rosengren tossed in three baskets from mid-range. Gary Anderson made a long shot from the top of the key. Bjorkman dribbled around the Halstad players and drew fouls in the process. When the dust settled, the Prowlers had outscored the Halstad Pirates by 20-6 in the third quarter and had taken a 43-36 lead. Thief River fans sat back with relief. Finally, their team had shown up and played their game. Halstad, now in even deeper foul trouble, looked defeated.

Despite the disaster, Kerrigan stuck to his strategy throughout the dismal third quarter. He rotated Bernhagen in the line-up, where he quickly ran into foul trouble. Kerrigan then reached down to the seventh man on the bench, Marlyn Aanenson, a junior and an experienced player who had started as a ninth grader before health problems knocked him out of the starting line-up. Aanenson became Kerrigan's next hatchet man, quickly racking up four fouls, most of them on Roger Williamson, who wasn't much for shooting free throws.

Trailing by 7 points as they huddled after the third quarter, the Pirates were now in a prime position for one of Kerrigan's patented, obscenity-laced, motivational tirades, and that's just what they got. Kerrigan put the starters back in with instructions to give 'er hell, foul out if you have to. If Halstad was going down, it was going to be in a blaze of glory.

But the disaster for Halstad continued. Dick Bjorkman continued the shooting and dribbling exhibition he had put on in the third quarter, stealing the ball and shooting a layup, then popping in a jump shot from fifteen feet. Jump shots were showboat stuff in the early 1950s, and the Thief River Falls fans went bonkers. With the Prowlers leading by 11 points, only four minutes remained in the game. In desperation, Ray Kerrigan called a time out.

As the Thief River fans roared and the players headed for their huddles, it looked as if it was all over. Halstad had made a gallant run in the first half, but with all of its players but Serum and Hesby in foul trouble, including Jimmy Akason with four, the game was all but in the bag for the Prowlers. As he walked to the Thief River huddle with a big smile on his face, Thief River guard Dick Bjorkman found his father in the audience and gave him a big thumbs-up sign.

The victory would be particularly sweet for Dick Bjorkman's father Cliff. In the 1926 region final, the elder Bjorkman had missed a crucial shot in the final minutes and Thief River Falls lost to Moorhead 20-16. Cliff Bjorkman was haunted by the missed shot ever since. Redemption would come, the elder Bjorkman hoped, when his son starred in a region final victory twenty-six years later.

In their jubilation, the Thief River players couldn't resist getting in a few digs at the Halstad five. "You played a nice game, Jim," Roger Williamson said to Jimmy Akason. "Too bad you won't be going to the state tournament."

Another Prowler shouted, "Too bad, farm boys!"

In the balcony, Halstad fans sat stunned. Although the cheerleaders kept up their whooping out of duty and the players' girlfriends screamed for their honeys in desperation, little Clarence Stennes knew it was over. After following his heroes with rapt admiration for nearly all of his conscious existence, these next few minutes would be the last time he saw them on the court. Clarence felt particularly bad for Jimmy Akason, whose glorious career would end with a crushing defeat in a game which could so easily have gone the other way.

In the huddle, Kerrigan instructed the players to go into a full-court press and press hard. Stunned by Thief River's run, Kerrigan was more sober than he had been between quarters. But something else happened during the time out. Jimmy Akason and the boys had taken exception to the comments from Thief River's players. The calm, coolheaded boys from Halstad got good and mad. The Thief River celebration was premature, and it was an insult. Thief River seemed to have forgotten that they had more than three minutes of basketball left to play.

After the time-out, Halstad scored a quick basket, then went to the full-court press. It worked. The Prowlers couldn't get the ball across the half court. Morrie Holm stole the ball and scored, and Halstad pressed again. Again the Prowlers were frustrated. The tight quarters between the wall and the baseline at the end of the gym didn't help. With only three feet to spare, whoever inbounded the ball had his back to a brick wall and couldn't step back to get more room. Holm stole the ball once again, Thompson scored, and the Pirates pressed again, with the same result. Once again, Thief River couldn't get the ball to half court.

If they couldn't get the ball across the time line, the Prowlers couldn't stall, which is what they had planned. The third time Halstad pressed, it was Serum's turn to score. It was his first basket since his 5-basket run at the beginning of the game. In a matter of one minute of play, Thief River's lead was cut to 5 points and the momentum had switched over to Halstad.

Then, Jimmy Akason took over. With Halstad trailing by 2 and 2:45 remaining in the game, the Halstad warhorse sank two free throws to tie the game at 51. A few seconds later, Akason nailed a hook shot which gave Halstad a 53–51 lead. The Brick House was in bedlam.

Akason then committed his fifth foul, which removed him from the game. Halstad was now without its star and floor leader. In Akason's absence, big Roger Williamson would have one last say for the Prowlers. After scoring his 27th and 28th points of the game on a hook shot from the left side, a score which tied the game at 53, Roger Williamson drove hard towards the basket. Don Thompson lowered his shoulder right into the tall Thief River center. The whistle blew and the Thief River fans roared in anticipation of a free-throw opportunity for their main man. But referee John Conzemius put his hand behind his head to indicate that Williamson had charged. The Thief River crowd was irate. Williamson was out of the game, the first time he had fouled out all year. Now, both team's stars were out of the game. The score was tied with 1:15 left to play.

As Williamson walked to the sideline to a warm ovation from the entire arena, Jimmy Akason came out to meet him at center court and shake his hand. Little Clarence Stennes will never forget the gentlemanly gesture. It showed a measure of respect between two gladiators, one of whom—nobody knew yet who—would never play high school basketball again.

Don Thompson went to the line to shoot one foul shot. When Thompson was nervous, he tended to shoot his free throws underhanded.

"I just asked the good Lord to help me," Thompson says today.

Thompson's free throw needed the assistance. The underhanded toss bounced three times on the rim before it dropped in. Halstad led 54–53.

The last half of the fourth quarter had been a bad dream for Thief River.

"It was like we were swimming in molasses," said young fan Loiell Dyrud, who listened on the radio at home. "It was really a nightmare."

It just got worse. Although they needed only 1 point to tie, 2 to win, the Prowlers, now without their star, Roger Williamson, fell apart. Panic set in. Bjorkman tried to take over but missed two rushed jump shots. Gary Anderson missed an easy shot from five feet out. Reserve Gary Smith missed another from underneath. The last seconds were nerve-wracking for Halstad, as they couldn't seem to get the rebound, but the same seconds were even more frustrating for Thief River, as shot after shot refused to drop. Fans from both sides roared and groaned and screamed and held their heads in their hands, peering between their fingers at the chaotic scene on the floor. It was, as the *Thief River Falls Times* later wrote, a "tingling finish" to what the *Fargo Forum* would call a "torrid affair." Finally, Halstad got a hold of a rebound and called a time-out.

With a 1-point lead and time remaining on the clock, Halstad had to get the ball across the time line before the Pirates could stall out the final seconds. Kerrigan knew whose hands he wanted on the ball—those of veteran Darrel Hesby. Hesby was quick, sure-handed, and shifty.

"Get it to Hesby and let him take it across the line," Kerrigan said.

Once across the line, Kerrigan instructed Hesby to crouch down around the ball, hold it to his gut with both arms, and let the final seconds tick away.

It all went as Kerrigan planned. Hesby dribbled across the half-court line and immediately bent down over the ball. Thief River's Gary Anderson, the most muscular player on both teams, went after the ball with angry desperation and threw both Hesby and the ball out of bounds as the buzzer sounded. For once, Darrel Hesby didn't roll around the ground like he was half-killed. The game was over. Halstad had won.

The next minutes were a blur. Legend has it that rabid Wimpy Bernhagen, Chuck's brother, who had been seated in the balcony, was the first Halstad fan on the floor. Some suspect he jumped out of the balcony, but nobody recalls seeing him do so. It would have been a twelve-foot drop.

Jimmy Akason's Uncle Clarence, who made the long drive from Kelso, North Dakota, threw his hat in the air. He never got it back.

As Halstad fans streamed onto the court, the Thief River players wilted to the floor in agony. Among the first to reach the Thief River bench was the minister of Thief River's biggest Lutheran Church. Pastor Thompson knelt in front of Roger Williamson and said, "You be the man, Roger." Williamson tried to be strong.

Halstad's contingent went crazy. Janet Sulerud rushed out on the floor and planted a kiss on the cheek of her honey, Darrel Hesby. Jane Jorgenson found her sweetie Don Thompson and gave him a hug. Such demonstrations of affection might seem subdued today, but at the time public kisses were reserved for the ends of world wars. Or, it seems, for when your boys won the regional basketball title.

After the trophies were awarded, the celebration moved into the locker room. There was old, stuffed-shirt, superintendent Arnold Kittleson, in a suit, tie, and hat, smiling ear to ear. Darrel Hesby, always willing to push the bounds of propriety, pulled Kittleson's hat down over his ears. For once, Kittleson didn't mind an affront to his dignity. He walked around the locker room dazed, greeting the players, his hat scrunched almost over his eyes.

The revelry continued. On the student fan bus on the way back to Halstad, student Nancy Waite kissed every rider while the chaperones stood idly by. Young Gene Thompson, Don's younger brother, was on the bus and never forgot it.

While Halstad celebrated deliriously, on the Thief River side the postmortems began immediately. Pastor Thompson threw out his planned sermon for the next morning's service and preached directly to the solemn congregation about the previous night's game. Cliff Bjorkman comforted his son Dick by assuring him from his experience in 1926 that, "losing builds more character than winning."

Dick told the press that he had rushed his three last jump shots, "and that probably cost us the game." Decades later, when Don Thompson shopped at Dick Bjorkman's clothing store in Thief River Falls, Bjorkman would shake his head and say, "I just can't imagine how we could have lost that game."

Gary Anderson took the defeat worse than any of the

Prowler players, even though he wasn't aware that his father had lost $1,000 on the game. The athletic guard disappeared for ten days into the big woods east of town. His parents likely knew where he was—his father owned an unheated hunting cabin there—but nobody else had any idea. Gary Anderson needed a hiatus and he took one.

The headline in the *Thief River Falls Times* said, "Halstad Forces Prowler Quint to Walk the Plank." Recriminations circulated around town. Bjorkman had hogged the ball. The refs had favored Halstad—John Conzemius' charging call on Williamson was clear evidence. Bob Nick had run the wrong offense.

Things got so bad that columnist Huck Olson saw fit to insert a paragraph in the *Times* calling for the blame game to stop. According to Olson, the Thief River fans could take comfort in knowing that their team was the best team in the region—whereas Halstad simply had the best squad. What Olson meant was that nobody could top Thief River's starting five if the other team had to stick to five players of their own. But Halstad had the depth to use eight players with equal results from each, and that is what sank the Prowlers.

Olson's analysis was correct. Kerrigan's strategy of deploying one player after another to harass Williamson didn't stop the big man from scoring 28 points. However, this aggressive plan had in the end helped cause Williamson to foul out of the game. Although Halstad was by that time without its star player, Jimmy Akason, the Pirates without Jimmy Akason were better than Thief River Falls without Roger Williamson. Halstad had been used to playing without Akason. He had missed two games as recently as the subdistrict tournament. And, thanks to Halstad's aggressive style of play, Jimmy fouled out frequently during the season. But the Thief River Falls Prowlers had become dependent upon Williamson over the course of the season. He had, after all, scored more than half of their points.

When Williamson went down, "You could see the look of fear on their faces," said one eyewitness, describing the teammates Williamson left behind on the floor.

Halstad center Don Thompson's solid performance should not be overlooked. Thompson gave away four-and-a-half inches to Prowlers' center Roger Williamson, and it was assumed before the game that Thompson would be neutralized. Instead, the Pirate center scored 15 points before he sank Halstad's 54th and final point on a dramatic free throw. Thompson's 16 points led the scoring for Halstad. Shorter than three of the Thief River Falls starting five, Thompson once again proved that he could hold his own with any center in the area, even Williamson, who was considered one of the finest pivot men in the state. Kerrigan's years of tutoring his protégé had paid off.

If Halstad had lost the regional final, the Halstad fans would have been disappointed, but not crushed. Ray Kerrigan would have gone home satisfied with a season which had exceeded his stated goal of winning a district title. The graduating seniors would have been satisfied that they had taken Halstad farther than the Pirates had ever gone before. They had been the fan favorite in the region tournament and would have remained so even if big bad Thief River Falls had knocked them out.

But Halstad didn't lose. Favored Thief River Falls did. And according to Roger Williamson, talking about the loss fifty-five years later, "that game changed our life."

Williamson went on to the University of North Dakota and eventually received an appointment from Congressman Harold Hagen to the United States Naval Academy in Annapolis, Maryland. He flew jets in Vietnam. He served in several countries around the world as a military attaché. He rose to the rank of full colonel in the air force. After retiring from the military, he became a successful money manager, turning his long-time investing hobby into a full-time career. And yet, when asked to discuss Thief River Falls' loss to Halstad in the district final, Williamson becomes somber.

His best friend, Gary Anderson, took it hard. Gary is now gone, a victim of stomach cancer. Bjorkman never got over it. He died of bone cancer in 2005. Bobo Dicken is gone. So is Tygeson. And every time Williamson returns to his old hometown, that loss to Halstad is topic number one. When he returned in the summer of 2007 for his fifty-fifth class reunion, he agreed to discuss the loss to Halstad in 1952.

The plane from Denver to Fargo was full, but it wasn't difficult to pick out a six-foot-five retired air force colonel from the passengers disembarking at Gate 2 at Hector Airport. Dignified and svelte, Williamson fit the part of former basketball star and retired air force colonel to a tee.

After lunch, Williamson drove sixty-five miles to Mahnomen, Minnesota, to visit the home of his opposite in the 1952 game, Halstad center Don Thompson. The two shook hands enthusiastically in Thompson's driveway and went inside to reminisce at the kitchen table for well over an hour. Don Thompson's sweetheart Jane, to whom he has been married for nearly fifty-five years, served open-faced sandwiches on homemade buns. The two old centers swapped stories about their teammates and coaches, about the game, and about their lives since. Both of them have lost an inch in height since high school. That's what seventy-three years will do to you.

Late in the conversation, Williamson became serious. "I want you to know," he said to Don Thompson, "that we were very proud of you. You represented us well in the state tournament."

"Thank you," Don Thompson replied, with a grateful nod of the head. The silence which followed was more profound than awkward. That game in Thief River Falls fifty-five years ago, a contest which lasted little more than an hour, still reverberated in the heads of two of its most notable participants as if it had happened yesterday.

Then things lightened up a bit. Roger Williamson told about his cousin Allan Williamson who had been a rabid fan of the Prowler team in 1952. He was still following basketball at his home in Wisconsin, having attended forty-seven Wisconsin State Basketball Tournaments in a row. The elder cousin had been recently diagnosed with a mild form of dementia that made him more blunt, more talkative, and more combative than the quiet gentleman he had been before. A sad situation, of course, but one which caused Allan Williamson to develop an impish sense of humor. He took to calling Roger frequently, usually to rehash old basketball games, and often to rehash one game in particular.

"Is this Roger?" Allan Williamson would say.

"Yes, this is Roger," his younger cousin would reply, knowing just what was coming.

And then Allan would crow, "This is Jimmy Akason!"

Meanwhile, Lincoln High band director Bob Harmon recovered well from his missed prediction. He successfully picked the other seven regional winners, which was quite a feat considering that three of them were considered upsets. And he didn't stay band director for long. After moving to New York City to sell Cadillacs, Harmon started his own football prediction business. The Bob Harmon Football Forecast is to this day the official college football predictor used by CBS Sports.

Coach Ray Kerrigan in a school photo found in center Don Thompson's scrapbook.

Halstad sports godfather and town-team baseball manager Erwin Warner in his baseball uniform.

Halstad coaches Kerrigan and Macleod are hoisted in the air by their players after the Pirates' unlikely defeat of Thief River Falls in the region VIII final in 1952.

Reserve Curt Johnson stands in front of Sulerud Hardware, which closed for the state basketball tournament in March, 1952.

Although Halstad center Don Thompson, right, lived in town, a *Minneapolis Star* photographer tracked him down at a farm outside of Halstad and asked him to pose with a horse, "Trigger," left.

In a posed picture for a Minneapolis paper, Reserve Don Lervold helps guard Morrie Holm with his tie before the two "head out for a stroll" at the state basketball tournament.

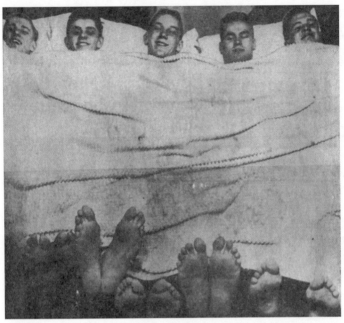

Left to right, Morrie Holm, Chuck Bernhagen, Dale Serum, Jim Akason and Don Thompson "relax" in the Curtis Hotel. Photo by the Fargo Forum.

Frank Steenerson, left, and Don Lervold "smiling after a cool shower" in a picture by a Minneapolis paper.

A Minneapolis paper poses Don Thompson, Albert Olson, and Darrel Hesby "relaxing" at the Curtis Hotel.

Coach Ray Kerrigan, left, poses for a Minneapolis paper with Assistant Coach Larry Macleod, right.

Minneapolis newspapermen posed Halstad reserve Marlyn Aanenson watching television for the first time, gawking at Williams Arena, and here, taking his first ride on an escalator.

Lt. Norris Johnson, who hitchhiked by air from Waco, Texas, to watch his home town play, is calling his brother. Watching him are Jimmy Akason, center, and Chuck Bernhagen.

Reserve Don Lervold "relaxes" in a photo published in the *Minneapolis Star*.

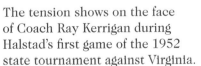

The tension shows on the face of Coach Ray Kerrigan during Halstad's first game of the 1952 state tournament against Virginia.

The tiny Halstad Band whoops it up at Williams
Arena in Minneapolis.

Halstad cheerleader Lois Johnson is captured by a *Minneapolis
Tribune* photographer in various states of distress.

Halstad guard Morrie Holm (4) goes up for a layup while Virginia's Dan Maryland (25) and Warren Sims (30) defend. Notice the height of the basketball floor relative to the fans in the front row.

Dale Serum (3) drives followed by Virginia's Rodney Hanson (21) and teammate Jim Akason (13).

Halstad center Don Thompson drives to the basket, watched by teammates Morrie Holm (4) and Dale Serum (3), as well as Virginia's Dan Maryland (25) and Bill Wirtnanen (26).

Virginia's Rodney Halven goes up for a layup with Halstad's Jim Akason following.

In a posed picture which was not far from reality, Halstad superintendent Arnold Kittleson is mobbed for tickets after Halstad wins the first round of the 1952 Minnesota State Boy's Basketball tournament.

Halstad mayor C. J. Hastad asks his father A. M. Hastad, president of Halstad's school board, for tickets in a picture set up by the *Minneapolis Star.*

Austin's basketball team was led by twin All-Staters Dayle and Don Rasmussen, guards who stood 5'6".

Coach Ray Kerrigan, left, beams at state tournament baseball hero Morrie Holm.

Ace Morrie Holm, left, and catcher Dale Serum, right, formed the Halstad Pirate's battery during much of the 1952 season.

The tired Halstad Pirates pose for a team photo after winning the state baseball tournament in June of 1952.

Part of the Halstad Pirate baseball team poses in front of the fire truck which met them on the way into town as the boys returned from the tournament in Owatanna. Remaining team members were in a car that got lost in Minneapolis and didn't return for another hour.

Halstad's high school Pirates baseball team on the way to the state tournament. Photo by Rusty Hastad.

A tired Morrie Holm, returning home as an Iron Man hero, poses for the *Norman County Index* in a photo taken at Four Mile Corner south of Halstad and west of Ada.

Dignitaries at the Halstad Lutheran Church banquet honoring the basketball team included, left to right: Assistant Pirate coach Larry Macleod, head coach Ray Kerrigan, Concordia College football coach Jake Christianson, keynote speaker Pastor Loyal Tallakson, Rev. Carl Opsahl and Concordia coach Vern Grinaker.

Right to left, Jim Akason, Darrel Hesby, George Johnson, and Don Thompson dig into the meal served by the Ladies Aid of the Halstad Lutheran Church at the celebration dinner held for the basketball team.

The Starting Five meet at the apartment home of Cora Stennes in Halstad in July of 2005. Back row, left to right: Jim Akason, Don Thompson, and Darrel Hesby. Front row, Morrie Holm, left; Dale Serum, right.

Chapter 9

Added Glory

The Halstad Masons had previously scheduled a recognition event for Halstad athletes to be held the Monday before the state basketball tournament. Given the unexpected victory over Thief River and the impending state tournament trip, the banquet was quickly turned into a celebration for the basketball team. Farmer D. E. Viker, a Mason, donated 130 pounds of turkey. Mrs. Albert Peterson prepared the meal, which had a St. Patrick's Day theme. Shamrocks decorated the tables. The speaker, Mr. John Brady of Mayville State Teachers College across the river in North Dakota, spoke on friendship.

"Several commented on his talk being one of the finest for young boys that they have heard," reported the *Valley Journal*.

Ray Kerrigan, Larry Macleod, and Jimmy Akason responded on behalf of the team. Superintendent Arnold Kittleson also gave remarks. Fifty boys and fifty men were served at the stag affair. It was to be the first of many such banquets held for the now-famous Halstad Pirates of 1952. But the rest of the celebrations would have to wait until the state tournament was in the books.

In the years following World War II, the Minnesota State Basketball Tournament was the biggest event of the Minnesota winter. Thanks in part to the size of the old Williams Arena on the campus of the University of Minnesota, Minnesota's state tournament outdrew any high school tournament in the nation. Although Williams Arena held up to 18,000 people, tickets for the state tournament were sold out months in advance, far before it was determined which teams would compete.

Some of the increase in high school basketball's popularity following the war could be attributed to changes in the game itself. When high school basketball first started in the 1910s, the game was fast, reckless, and undisciplined. Many teams, including Fosston, who won the first state championship in 1913, didn't have a coach. What few coaches there were had a simple philosophy: Let the boys play.

In the late 1920s, the first crop of trained coaches came out of college bearing their physical education degrees. They brought discipline to the court. They also subscribed to a generally held belief of the time that running fast on a hard floor was detrimental to bone development in young boys. So, the coaches slowed the game down to a yawn-inducing crawl. Scores of 21–10 were the norm.

Archaic rules also slowed the game down. Through the 1920s, infractions such as traveling or losing the ball out-of-bounds resulted in time-consuming free throws rather than a mere change of possession. Until 1937, every basket was followed by a jump ball at center court. In addition to the stately pace dictated by the rules, in the 1920s a sedate, "midwestern" style of basketball developed which emphasized ball control and passing. Dribbling the ball was a sign of poor teamwork. True teams found a way to pass the ball up court without its ever touching the floor. If a team decided that it was in its best interest to stall, the game could simply grind to a halt.

According to the book *Minnesota Hoops*, two events in the 1940s went a long ways towards making the game more exciting. The first event took place at the 1944 state tournament when six-foot-seven-inch Jim McIntyre of Minneapolis Patrick Henry High School played his first game on the floor of Williams Arena. Old-school types were enraged as Patrick Henry's strategy became evident: Feed it to the big guy and let him dump it in the basket. Oddly, the idea of using the tallest man on the floor to score the bulk of the baskets was seen as dirty pool. But it worked, and soon basketball coaches all over Minnesota combed the classrooms of their schools for tall boys, however unathletic and gawky, whom they could turn into basket-scoring machines.

Thief River Falls had found Roger Williamson, already a good athlete, and once he learned to shoot with both hands he scored over half of the team's points. In Halstad, Ray Kerrigan had fewer options. All he could come up with for a center was six-foot-one-inch Don Thompson, a good athlete on the football field but one without any apparent proclivity for basketball. At barely six feet, he was the tallest player they had. Kerrigan, and later Larry Macleod, taught Thompson to pivot both ways and score with his left hand as well as his right.

The same story was repeated hundreds of times in Minnesota high schools. But the eternal search for the big guy didn't happen until after big Jim McIntyre showed how it was done in the state tournament of 1944.

The second event which changed the game was the appearance at Williams Arena of the Lynd, Minnesota, team of 1946, a team which practiced in the loft of a barn. Tiny Lynd wasn't the first Cinderella team in state tournament history. In fact, "darling" teams from small schools had won the state title for five consecutive years from 1939–1944. But Lynd became a sensation for how they played: They ran a fast break from the opening buzzer to the final bell. Such a style of play had not been seen much since well before 1920. The fast-break offense concerned the physical education types who worried about destroying boys' bones, but it thrilled the crowd at Williams Arena into delirium.

Lynd eventually ran out of steam, losing 63–31 to mighty Austin in the 1946 championship game, but their style of play made them the overwhelming favorites of the Williams Arena crowd and the media. And one of the faces in that crowd, attending his first state tournament and soaking up every minute of it, was ten-year-old Jimmy Akason of Halstad.

The Lynd tournament appearance marked another change: Most of Lynd's players were farm boys. Up to 1946, it was common knowledge that farm boys didn't have time to go to high school, much less play basketball. The city newspapers seized upon the story of the Lynd farm boys upsetting the big city boys.

The urban journalists missed the larger point: Farming had changed since the war. As mentioned, Lynd practiced in a barn loft. That meant the barn loft was empty of hay. So were hundreds of barn lofts in the Minnesota countryside. Many farmers had sold their dairy cows to go into less labor-intensive crop farming during the war.

With the larger machinery, fewer hands were needed on the farm. For the first time since settlement, farm boys not only wanted to continue their education beyond the eighth grade, but they also had time to play a little ball. And they were good at it.

So, when Halstad showed up at the state tournament in 1952, the Minneapolis newspapermen had their scripts written in advance. Halstad was 1952's darling. Like Lynd, Halstad was a tiny town. Like Lynd's team, the Pirates were farm boys, or so read the script. In fact only one of Halstad's Starting Five, Morrie Holm, actually lived on a farm, but because the script had already been written, the other Pirates were turned into farm boys as well.

When Halstad beat Thief River Falls to earn a berth in the state tournament, the immediate problem for Pirate fans was getting tickets. Out of the 18,000 seats in Williams Arena, Halstad was allotted only one hundred seats due to the size of its school. Superintendent Arnold Kittleson was faced with the impossible task of distributing the one hundred tickets to the many hundreds of people identified with Halstad who wanted to attend the games. When the tickets went on sale in Kittleson's office, a line formed which stretched outside the school into the March cold.

The *Fargo Forum* claimed Superintendent Arnold Kittleson had up to 1,000 ticket requests to fill. In the end, at least 400 people came to the tournament from up north, in addition to the former Halstad residents who came from other areas of the country. Newspapers reported that former Halstad resident Herman Helleloid would be flying in from California to see the tournament.

Norris Johnson, a Halstad graduate in the service in Texas, asked his commander for a seven-day leave.

"He asked me, 'What for?'" Johnson told a Minneapolis newspaper. "I said, 'Colonel, I would like to go to Minnesota to a basketball game.' He said, 'Johnson, you've always been a little wacky.'"

The normally unflappable Kittleson was in a bind.

"I keep having visions of people from all over the United States descending upon me for tickets," he told a reporter. "If they win the first game, I am going to just leave town. That's all. I am going to just leave town."

After the Thief River game ended and the celebration on the court simmered down, many Halstad people piled into the restaurants in Thief River Falls for a late- night snack before the long trip home to Halstad. A few Thief River fans who had purchased tickets in anticipation of going to the tournament in Minneapolis themselves showed up at the cafes and either sold or simply gave their tickets to the Halstad fans. But regional affiliation was strong. Once you lost out, you pulled for the team from your area until they, too, were defeated. In fact, many Thief River fans went down to the state tournament despite their team's galling loss to Halstad.

One newspaper account alleged that in the chaotic swirl for tickets, Kittleson himself had taken a financial hit. The allegation is scoffed at by Halstad residents today. Arnold Kittleson, they argue, was as tight as they came. The books for the Halstad school were always correct right down to the penny. Kittleson squeezed every dime in the school budget, and he squeezed every dime in his household budget.

As kindly as Kittleson and his wife were, the meals served at luncheons at the Kittleson household tended to emphasize inexpensive ingredients. Jell-O® with nothing in it. Hot dishes long on noodles and short on meat. In fact, Mrs. Kittleson was known to purchase wieners at the grocery store three at a time. So, there is just no way, according to longtime Halstad residents, that old Arnold Kittleson lost a dime on tickets for the state tournament. But the story wouldn't die.

The one hundred tickets given to Halstad by tournament organizers were in one block. The band, students, and close relatives of the players and the coaches sat in that cluster. The other estimated 450 people who attended the tournament from the Halstad area were spread throughout the huge arena. Added to that number were about 200 former Halstad residents who had moved to the Twin Cities. Together, as impressive as they were in number when one considers Halstad's population of 595, they barely made a dent in Williams Arena and couldn't have made enough noise to be noticed.

It didn't matter. Little Halstad was the tournament darling. From the opening whistle, the bulk of the crowd was boisterously—even obnoxiously—behind the Pirates. Instead of being out-shouted by the other thousands, Halstad supporters from all over the state dominated the arena to the point where the crowd support for the larger towns Halstad opposed sounded downright anemic. The crowd's rabid support for Halstad, a team they had never watched before, even extended to booing the opposing team during introductions, something some Halstad fans remember with embarrassment.

Going to state. The smaller the town, the more magic the words. To fifth grader Clarence Stennes, it was unimaginable. The fame! the glory! To think he walked the same halls as those guys, the Starting Five. It was heady stuff for Clarence, for all the students at the Halstad school, and for every resident of the little town on the Minnesota prairie.

Aside from the thrill of watching a good team, going to state gives small-town residents hope for an end to their anonymity. For twenty years afterwards, when somebody asks where you're from and you say, "Halstad," instead of saying, "Never heard of it," the sophisticated city person you are trying to impress might squint their eyes and dimly remember hearing about your basketball team. If you are from a small town, such recognition is priceless. It can break the ice at the opening of a frightening job interview. It is the difference between being a nobody, a complete hick, and being from someplace that matters.

Within a few days after the Pirates qualified for the state tourney, a Halstad resident who was traveling in southern Minnesota reported getting stopped by the police for speeding.

When the officer saw the driver's town of origin, he said, "Isn't that the little town that just got into the state tournament?"

Indeed it was. The driver got off with a verbal warning and hearty congratulations from the policeman. And the incident appeared in the *Valley Journal*.

If you haven't grown up in a small town, it is difficult

to understand the mix of pride and shame that coming from a small town engenders. Pride, because you love the old hometown and its characters and because you can't imagine a more fun place to grow up. Shame, because nobody else seems to realize how wonderful your hometown is. They're all proud of their hometowns, or they live in the city where nobody seems to be proud of anything but how much money they're making.

As a result, small-town residents cling to anything which might give them some sense of significance, some way of becoming known to the world at large. Until 1952, Halstad residents had little to hang their hat on—unless you count Skitch Henderson. Before 1952, the famous musician and bandleader was Halstad's main claim to fame. However, there were complications.

Lyle Henderson was born in Halstad and, after he was orphaned at a young age, Lyle was raised there by his Aunt Hattie Gift. Aunt Hattie was gifted musically, and she taught young Lyle everything she knew, even though the kid fought her tooth and nail to avoid practicing. When he finally got around to it, he could play anything on the piano, and he could write songs as well. Later, Skitch Henderson (a name which was supposedly given to Henderson by Bing Crosby because the pianist could "sketch" a song in any key) would credit his persistent

Aunt Hattie with "giving me everything I had." But at the time young Lyle was anything but appreciative.

After performing throughout the Midwest, Skitch was offered a contract with NBC. When he signed the contract, he was asked to list his hometown. Instead of putting down Halstad, Skitch or his publicist—depending upon who you believe—listed his birthplace as Birmingham, England. Skitch later explained to relatives that his change of birthplace was simply to further his career. Birmingham sounded more glamorous than Halstad. Who, after all, had ever come from Halstad, Minnesota?

Skitch Henderson went on to big success in the music world. He performed with Bob Hope and Bing Crosby. He was Johnny Carson's first bandleader on the Tonight Show. He founded the New York Pops Orchestra, which he based out of Carnegie Hall.

But throughout his distinguished career, Skitch Henderson turned his back on Halstad. Instead of withdrawing his spurious claim to having been born in England, Henderson expanded upon it. Not only was he born in Birmingham, but he was educated in Switzerland. He studied with legendary German composer Arnold Shoenberg. He joined the Royal Air Force and fought in the Battle of Britain. Then, he "switched over" to the

American air force and came to this country, where he finished out his military duties and started a musical career by touring the Midwest.

It was all a pack of lies. It is certain that Henderson was born in Halstad, not Birmingham. His birth records survive in Norman County, as do pictures of the young dandy Lyle in a cape on the lawn of a Halstad home with his friend Olga Gilbertson. Plus, there are a raft of Henderson relatives around Halstad who remember him and who haven't taken kindly to Skitch's writing them and their town out of his past.

Henderson did return to Halstad once. One day just after the war, he made a low pass over Halstad in a plane. Young Roger Stole remembers walking home from school for lunch and thinking that the town was getting strafed. But Henderson's pass over Halstad was meant to alert a relative to his arrival. Skitch's plane then landed on a highway outside of town, and Henderson was ferried into Halstad.

Within an hour, classes at the school were dismissed and students were instructed to meet in the gym. A piano was rolled in and Henderson gave an impromptu concert. Afterwards, he went uptown and met with locals at the cafe. As far as anybody knows, it was the last time Henderson came home.

In the 1970s, Henderson's tendency to embellish caught up with him. The IRS prosecuted him for lying about the value of a donation of manuscripts he made to the University of Wisconsin. Composers Leonard Bernstein and Henry Mancini had valued the collection at $350,000, Henderson claimed, citing documents which were eventually found to be forged. Both celebrities denied anything of the sort, and Henderson spent a year in prison for tax evasion.

Henderson continued to maintain his lies about his past until his death in 2005. His obituary in the *New York Times* repeats Henderson's fabricated biography as undisputed fact, even though even Henderson's military service in the United States is in some doubt.

"Cheap lies," says Skitch's first cousin, Harris Henderson, now 96 years old and a resident of the Lutheran Memorial Home in Halstad. "Why he had to go in for such cheap lies."

The bitterness in Halstad towards Skitch Henderson is a result of the small-town desire to cling to something, anything, which will give them some greater identity, some sense of renown. That thirst explains why it is a picture of the Halstad basketball team of 1952, not a picture of Skitch Henderson, which hangs on the wall of

Halstad's lone remaining cafe in the year 2007. Unlike Skitch, those boys didn't deny their roots. The distinguished basketball team of 1952 let the Halstad folks come along for the ride. So many people made the trip to Minneapolis for the tournament that the Halstad school closed Tuesday afternoon for the rest of the week. So did Sulerud Hardware and many other downtown businesses. The PTA meeting was canceled, as was the Ladies Aid meeting. The *Norman County Index* reported that electricity consumption in the town of Halstad dropped from the usual average of 3490 KWH to 2760 KWH on the first day of the tournament. At the same time, the phone switchboard in Halstad had never done such business.

"If the Halstad Telephone office ever needed a two-position board it was during these days of preparation for the state tournament," wrote the *Valley Journal*.

The costs of bringing the team to the tournament were borne by the Minnesota State High School League, but the band had to raise its own money for the trip. With the support of local businesses, $1,000 was raised in a single day. Decimated by the loss of the basketball players, the band's ace trumpet player, Paul Opsahl, said their attempt to make noise was lost in the rafters of Williams Arena, but "we played our hearts out."

The band had a good time seeing Minneapolis. A sheet handed out to the band members before they left town urged the students to check into the hotel in an orderly manner so they could go about exploring the city. "There are no rules at this time," the instruction sheet continued, a statement which seems incredible today.

"As far as I am concerned," wrote the director of the band, Lloyd Anderson, "you will be allotted as much liberty as you want. Let's all use our heads and I know that we will all have a good time."

Amidst the furor, Ray Kerrigan had to get his boys ready to play. To acclimate them to the new glass backboards which were coming in at the time, Kerrigan took the team down to Hendrum to practice in their new gym. The Hendrum gym had glass backboards of the same shape and size as those in Williams Arena. It was the only practice session the team would have between the Thief River victory and their departure for Minneapolis.

To the media, Kerrigan declaimed any hopes of doing much at the tournament. Indeed, pretournament newspaper prognostications, and there were many, gave Halstad little chance. Today, the players don't remember harboring any dreams of state tournament success. They listened to their coach and all he ever told them was to do their best. Whatever the Halstad Pirates did at the state tournament, Kerrigan told a reporter, was merely "added glory."

However, it is impossible to believe that Ray Kerrigan didn't harbor dreams of making waves in Minneapolis. He was too much the competitor. He recognized the chance of a lifetime when he saw one. And he did what he could to prepare the team.

There were media distractions before the team left for Minneapolis, even in Halstad. The *Minneapolis Tribune* sent up a reporter and a photographer. The *Fargo Forum* and other regional newspapers came to town. Inevitably, players were asked to pose with their favorite farm animals. Morrie Holm held a sheep. Marlyn Aanenson was pictured with his dog.

Don Thompson lived in town, but he was pictured in the *Minneapolis Tribune* in his fur cap holding the reins of a horse allegedly named Trigger. To this day, Don Thompson can't figure out where they found that horse, or whose horse it was, or where they took the picture. He had never owned a horse in his life. Turns out, according to Thompson's younger brother Gene, the horse was owned by a farmer on the edge of town whom Thompson was visiting when the newspapermen tracked him down.

The gregarious Ray Kerrigan was happy to absorb most of the media attention. He professed his relative ignorance of the game, gave credit to assistant Larry Macleod for bringing in his expertise, bragged about the athleticism of his boys, and gave credit to the coach at his alma mater, St. Olaf College, without mentioning that he never played a minute of basketball at the school. Kerrigan played trumpet in the renowned St. Olaf band.

Erwin Warner, Arnold Kittleson, and Ray Kerrigan drove the team to Minneapolis in their own cars. They were scheduled to stop in Anoka to practice on a big floor before heading into the big city to face the media circus. However, by the time they found the gym, they only had enough time to stretch out their legs before piling back into the cars for the remainder of the trip.

As was tournament custom, Halstad, as the team which drove the farthest, was the first team to arrive at the Curtis Hotel in downtown Minneapolis. They were greeted by dozens of photographers and reporters. The team ran a gauntlet of blinding flashbulbs and, according to Darrel Hesby, pushy reporters asking "dippy questions" as they entered the hotel. No matter how they answered the dippy questions, the reporters did what they liked with their quotes, embarrassing those who made the mistake of giving their name out by misquoting them to fit their story. Sheltered, starry-eyed farm boys come to the big city!

The morning after they arrived, the Pirates toured Williams Arena. Reporters trailed, trolling for quotes which they could turn into grist for their mill. Coach Kerrigan was along on the tour, and he was in a boisterous mood. As they walked into the arena, he turned to good-natured reserve Marlyn Aanenson, who was about as much of a farm boy as anybody on the Halstad team, and cracked that the arena "sure could hold a lot of hay." A reporter seized on the quote, confirmed Aanenson's farm-boy credentials, and pulled him away from the team. Aanenson was then dragged around downtown Minneapolis with a photographer for an endless series of posed pictures.

The next day's *Minneapolis Star* featured a full-page photo spread of humble, quiet Marlyn Aanenson. The headline: "Yes, Marlyn, this place would hold a lot of hay."

Beneath the headline was a giant picture of the interior of Williams Arena with a dwarfed Marlyn Aanenson standing alone far below.

The story didn't stop there. Here we have Marlyn riding an escalator. His alleged comment: "A fella could get lazy riding one of these!" Here Marlyn is gazing into his first television set, as if mesmerized. Another huge photo shows Marlyn in his farm hat, gawking at a skyscraper. Supposedly he said, "These buildings are pretty tall if you look up at them for a while!" The reporter had turned Marlyn Aanenson into a celebrity hick.

For many years after, Ray Kerrigan felt bad about the crack he made to Marlyn Aanenson about the arena holding a lot of hay. He didn't intend for the reporter to turn it into such a spread. Kerrigan wondered to his daughter later how all the fame had affected the quiet farm boy.

But shy, reserved, good-humored Marlyn Aanenson wasn't traumatized by his celebrity status. Fifty-five years later, he remembers his notoriety with good humor. The state tournament was his first trip to the city, after all, he said. And it was the first television set he had ever set eyes on.

Aanenson also pointed out that he was only a reserve on the basketball team. A few months later, Halstad's high school baseball team would make its own mark with slick-fielding Marlyn Aanenson starting at first base.

"That's what I am most proud of," Aanenson said. Coach Kerrigan needn't have worried.

Unlike Marlyn Aanenson, most of the Halstad team had been to Minneapolis before. Although Jimmy Akason had been the first to see a state tournament basketball game, in 1946, he later added other teammates to the trip. Oddly, it seems they were never chaperoned. They never missed a game, but that doesn't mean they were angels. It became a tradition for the boys to hit the Alvin Burlesque Theater for a show, quite a risqué thing for a bunch of small-town boys at the time. Jimmy Akason, who looked twenty years old from the time he was twelve, never had trouble getting in the door. For some of the others, it was a stretch. But times were different.

"If you could reach up high enough to push your quarter across the counter, they'd let you in," said Darrel Hesby.

During their junior year, there had been no trip to the Alvin Burlesque Theater. Ray Kerrigan had taken several of the boys down to the 1951 state tournament in his car, and he wasn't of a mind to put up with nonsense of the burlesque theater sort. However, at the hotel one evening as they were kicking back and shooting the breeze between tournament games, Kerrigan had let slip a crazy idea.

"Next year, boys," he said, "we come down to play."

At the time, everybody had laughed.

The Curtis Hotel, eventually razed in the 1980s, was

an institution in Minneapolis. It occupied a city block. It was the high-class place to stay for country folks who came to the big city, and for people from around the world who visited Minneapolis.

Every March, the Curtis became the headquarters of the Minnesota State Boys Basketball Tournament. To make sure the teams were on an even footing, all players were required to stay at the Curtis during the tourney, even if their home was just down the street. To players from far away, staying at the Curtis with its luxurious pool surrounded by live palm trees and tropical vegetation was almost as glamorous as playing in the tournament itself. To coaches of teams from the metropolitan area, however, staying at the Curtis was an unnecessary distraction, an irritating sop to the outstate hicks. "Outstate," by the way, is a word people in the Minneapolis/St. Paul metro area use to this day to describe the entire remaining population of Minnesota.

As the Halstad boys settled in their rooms at the Curtis, they still couldn't fend off photographers. No fewer than three different newspapers took a posed picture of five team members under the blankets of their bed with their toes sticking out. More front-page exposure, this time of the Pirates' bare feet.

One picture showed reserve Don Lervold helping Morrie Holm tie his tie in their room at the Curtis before they "headed out for a stroll." A painfully posed picture showed the Halstad coaches "plotting strategy." Arnold Kittleson was shown on the phone managing ticket requests, a photo which at least bore some semblance to reality. A beaming Frankie Steenerson and Don Lervold were pictured with water pouring over their heads while showering after practice—the obvious implication being that a shower was quite a novelty for boys used to a Saturday evening bath in the old washtub.

As they walked the halls of the Curtis, several Halstad boys ran into players from Virginia, Halstad's first-round opponent. The Virginia boys made it clear that they intended to win the entire tournament and Halstad wasn't going to stand in their way.

Darrel Hesby recalls being more puzzled than angry. Going to the tournament was an overwhelming thrill. To him, playing the actual games would be a bonus, something he hadn't worried much about. It seemed odd to Hesby that a team would come in hell-bent to win the thing. Weren't the Virginia boys just glad to be part of the fun?

Of course, some Halstad fans had to stay behind in the old hometown. Not everybody could afford to go.

Some of the fathers of the players were too busy with work to attend. For those from Halstad who couldn't make the drive down to Minneapolis and for the thousands of basketball fans in the northwestern corner and western edge of Minnesota who were familiar with Ray Kerrigan, Jimmy Akason, and the Pirates of Halstad, the game would be carried by KVOX radio in Moorhead.

KVOX's primary sportscaster was Manny Marget. An excitable, opinionated sort, Marget's dry, no-nonsense broadcasting style, interspersed with occasional barbs and slightly off-color cracks, made him a popular institution in the Red River Valley.

However, Marget had not yet seen the Halstad Pirates play. He viewed their ascension to the state tournament as a fluke. He expressed on the air his opinion that it was unfortunate that Region 8 hadn't sent a better representative to the Big Show in Minneapolis. Marget would broadcast the Halstad games at Williams Arena, but he made it clear that he thought the trip was going to be a waste of his time.

Manny Marget's opinion would soon change.

Chapter 10

Drama at the Barn

It is always a blessing to be underestimated, but sometimes you are underestimated for a reason. Although the Halstad Pirates were identified as the state tournament "darling" before they even arrived in Minneapolis, nobody had much hope that they would make a mark in Minneapolis. The main concern was the Halstad team's notable lack of height. Although the tournament program listed five Halstad players at six feet, somebody somewhere was being generous. Only Don Thompson, at six-feet and one-half inch, exceeded the six-foot mark. And Virginia, Halstad's first-round opponent, had four starters over six-feet-two-inches. It would be an uphill battle for the Pirates.

Ray Kerrigan had no idea what to expect from Virginia. He had no scouting reports on the boys from the Iron Range, and he sought out none. His strategy remained simple: Stick to our style of play and let the chips fall where they may. If things go well, it will simply be "added glory."

Williams Arena could intimidate teams who had

never played there before. Beside the obvious matter of the 18,000 screaming fans, there was the floor. It was raised. To the first row of fans and to both benches, the floor was at chest height. Some players had a tough time getting over the sensation that they were going to slide off the side and get hurt.

Then there were the baskets. Every basket the Halstad team had seen up to this point had hung from the end wall of a gym. At Williams Arena, the baskets stuck out on the end of long poles. And the backboards at Williams were made of glass, another novelty for the Pirates. They had played one game with a glass backboard, that back in January in Valley City, North Dakota.

"It was a little different than playing in Borup," Dale Serum says today.

In the end, none of the usual problems bothered the players, but one quirk of Williams Arena was an unpleasant surprise: the wooden raised court had soft spots. On certain areas of the court, the ball would go dead. To a team used to tile floors, dribbling on the dead spots was the biggest problem at Williams Arena.

From the opening buzzer, at least 15,000 of the 18,000 paying customers were rabidly pro-Halstad. Recordings of the radio broadcast confirm that Halstad could do no wrong. Every one of their successes brought a chilling roar, and every call that went against the Pirates brought a chorus of boos. But the players recall hearing nothing, once they were on the floor.

The press watched the Halstad boys closely to see if they were at all intimidated, either by their Virginia opponents, by the large crowd, or by the unfamiliar court. They soon got their answer. After both Jimmy Akason and Morrie Holm missed easy layups to start the game, Akason looked over at Holm and grinned as if to say, "No big deal, we'll get the next ones."

Jimmy Akason was anything but uptight. The press reported Akason's confident smile widely in the next morning's newspapers. The game, according to the *Minneapolis Tribune*, "had none of the jitters and erratic play which usually mark the first contest of a state tournament."

Kerrigan went with Bernhagen, Holm, Akason, Thompson, and Serum to start the game. After the two missed layups, Thompson shot three baskets from close in. Halstad, after trailing Virginia 3–2, took the lead 6–3. The Pirates' free-lance offense did what it did all year and went with the hot hand. After Thompson's burst of baskets, Virginia adjusted their defense. Then it was

Bernhagen's turn, and then Akason's. Halstad led at the end of the first quarter by a score of 21–16. Although both teams were shooting unusually well, Halstad had the higher percentage—an unheard of 58 percent—in the first half.

In the broadcast booth, Manny Marget was having a change of heart. After introducing the line-ups with stern professionalism and describing the first minutes of the game in flat tones, Marget's enthusiasm for the Halstad team started to build.

"These guys are fighters!" he shouted in the middle of the second quarter after Halstad's Morrie Holm had once again stolen the ball from Virginia.

Then Jimmy Akason went on a roll. He couldn't miss. Marget was impressed. The final shot of Akason's run came when the Halstad veteran worked up too much steam as he headed down the court. In desperation, he jumped into the air under the basket at the out-of-bounds line and hooked the ball high in the general direction of the basket. The shot went over the backboard and some-how went in. The crowd let loose the biggest roar of the game. Manny Marget, who thought it was a designed play, couldn't believe it. He was a convert. By the end of the first half, at which point Halstad led 39–32, Marget announced, "Of course, we're pulling for Halstad!"

The crowd exited the stands to go out to the concourse for halftime. Many of the 18,000-some fans went to have a cigarette. The smoke drifted back into the arena. It was sort of expected that the third quarter of every game in Williams would begin in a blue haze of tobacco smoke.

After falling behind by 11 points early in the third period, Virginia, led by center Warren Sims, forward Jack Stromberg, and tiny guard Don Maryland, stormed back. By the end of the third quarter, Virginia had cut the Halstad lead to 6 points.

Virginia's torrid shooting continued as the fourth quarter started. Stromberg cut the lead to 4 points with a jump shot. Hesby responded for Halstad by pumping in 2 from far out in the field. With four minutes remaining, Virginia stole the ball and scored to narrow the margin back to 4 points. Halstad was staggering. Virginia was charging.

Akason then fouled Sims, who made the first free throw to narrow the margin to 3. The Blue Devils elected to take the ball out of bounds on the second free throw, but Halstad stole the ball and Akason scored to give Halstad a 5-point lead with one minute to go.

Stromberg answered with a basket. As the Pirates

brought the ball back up, Virginia stole the ball. Don Maryland missed a layup, but Ron Halunen picked up the rebound and dumped it in to cut the Halstad lead to 1. In an attempt to foil Halstad's stall, Stromberg then fouled a Halstad player. Halstad elected to take the ball out of bounds rather than shoot the free throw. The Pirates intended to stall out the final seconds.

The stall failed when Chuck Bernhagen stepped over the half court line with seven seconds remaining in the game. Trailing by 1 point, Virginia had the ball out of bounds. Their plan was to get it to Jack Stromberg. The Virginia star worked his way to the basket, guarded by Jimmy Akason. In the chaos and crowd noise, Stromberg put up the last-second shot. It went in. But Jimmy Akason had heard the horn.

"Too late!" Akason yelled at referee Louis Fillipi.

"Too late!" agreed Fillipi, and the game was over.

Halstad won their first game of the state tournament by 1 point.

Virginia fans were furious. However, neither Jack Stromberg nor Virginia coach Art Stock argued the call. An overdramatized newspaper report the next day had Stromberg in tears, repeatedly telling his coach that he was sorry for putting the ball up late.

"The ref was right, coach! I didn't get that ball up in time!"

A more sober, and likely a more accurate, report quoted a somber Stromberg in the locker room.

"It wasn't a shot I ordinarily would have tried, but I didn't have time for anything else. I saw the clock and thought I better just let fly. But I knew it was too late."

Coach Kerrigan was ebullient as he took the rostrum in the locker room to face the press. He couldn't stand still. According to *Tribune* reporter Lou Gelfand, "Ray Kerrigan's clump of curly hair was literally jumping up and down." First, Kerrigan had to find a reporter with a cigarette. Then he turned to the team.

"Thanks for everything you've done, even though I gave you heck," he said. He told a reporter that Halstad was lucky. But then Kerrigan saw across the locker room that Chuck Bernhagen was down, still angry at himself for stepping across the half line and giving Virginia the ball with seven seconds to play. Kerrigan ran to whisper something in Bernhagen's ear before jumping back on the rostrum to address the throng of reporters.

"What a kid," he said of the sensitive Bernhagen. "He plays great defense just like he has all year and then he gets upset over a single mistake."

Then Kerrigan remembered something from the game, jumped off the rostrum, and ran into the shower to remind a player not to "go too deep on the guard around."

The press asked Akason about smiling at Holm after a missed layup.

"I thought it was kind of funny to miss such an easy one," he was reported as saying in the next morning's papers. The reporters also saw in the locker room that Jimmy Akason was still suffering from a hacking cough, which was probably not helped at all by the tobacco haze everywhere in Williams, including in the locker room. A University of Minnesota trainer gave Jimmy some cough syrup. Ray Kerrigan tried to grab the bottle to take a celebratory swig, but the trainer didn't allow it.

"It is okay during the day," Akason said of his cough, "but when I run it gives me trouble."

Thompson led the scoring for Halstad with 15. Akason followed with 12. Bernhagen chipped in 10. According to big Virginia center Warren Sims, "Thompson gave us some trouble until we adjusted our defense."

Thompson had faked out Sims enough early in the game that Virginia coach Art Stock had to abandon the man-to-man offense. Even so, Sims maintained, "Akason is their top player."

Virginia's guard Don Maryland pointed out to the press something nobody else noticed. After Bernhagen was called for the over-and-back violation, the score-keeper had let the clock run for three seconds before stopping it with seven seconds remaining. Those three seconds would have made the difference on Stromberg's final shot. Virginia would have won.

Halstad had shot 52 percent from the floor, and what the *St. Paul Pioneer Press* called an "astounding" 58 percent in the first half, a blistering percentage at the time. Virginia had used its height advantage to out-rebound Halstad by a 2–1 ratio, but Halstad made up the difference by repeatedly stealing the ball from the taller but slower Blue Devils. After taking the lead 4–3, Halstad never trailed.

Legendary Minnesota Gopher coach Ozzie Cowles took in the game. He was impressed by the Halstad shooting display, which was described by the *Minneapolis Tribune* as "the most sensational shooting exhibition" ever seen in tournament play.

"It is surprising," Cowles told *Tribune* reporter Sid Hartman, "how the kids come in and play on a strange big floor with a lot of space and shoot with such confidence despite the pressure."

Another columnist was impressed by the poise shown by Halstad's farm boys in the Virginia game. "Certainly, you no longer suspect that Halstad's cagers are small-town boys who came here merely to ride the street cars and look at television for the first time."

Again, Halstad's depth came into play. Kerrigan rotated Bernhagen, Hesby, and Aanenson into the line-up with good effect, while Virginia coach Art Stock used only his starting five to play the entire game. The game was cleaner than usual for the Pirates. Only 18 fouls were called between the two teams. The game was completed in just over one hour.

The Halstad vs. Virginia game was watched by a reported 18,961 fans at Williams Arena, although the number of spectators varies wildly from newspaper to newspaper. In any case, it was the largest crowd ever to have seen a high school basketball game in the United States at the time.

The newspapers in the Twins Cities now had their darling. Halstad's surprising victory topped the headlines the next morning. As one columnist pointed out, the crowd at the arena was thirty-two times larger than the entire town of Halstad.

Back home, Don Thompson's mother and father listened to the game on the radio. Mrs. Thompson was so proud she sat down with a pencil and wrote her son a letter.

"You should hear all the people rave," she wrote. "They think you guys are above the earth."

She noted that the siren sounded after Stromberg's shot was ruled no good. After reminding Don to bring home souvenirs for the younger kids, she added that some people were taking a plane down to Minneapolis for the next evening's game. The letter was addressed to Don Thompson, Halstad B. Ball player, Minneapolis, Minnesota (c/o Curtis Hotel). Mailed on Friday, it reached Don Thompson in room 318 at the Curtis Hotel the next morning.

Arnold Kittleson's fears were realized. Halstad had won the first round, and now the pressure for tickets for the semifinal against South St. Paul was even more intense than it had been for the first-round game. To add to Kittleson's problems, Halstad's allotment for the second game was reduced to 50, with more Halstad fans arriving by the minute. Kittleson called home to Halstad and asked the phone operator to pass the word around town that those who hadn't left yet should stay home and listen to the game on the radio. There was little chance that they would get in.

Ray Kerrigan sympathized and stood up for Kittleson in the press.

"There's nothing school officials can do about it. We know we'll be in bad with a lot of our townspeople, but that's all the tickets we have."

The *Fargo Forum* sent a reporter up to Halstad to check on how things were going back in the old hometown.

"Even third graders were crowded in here to listen to the radio," said Mrs. Imogene Peterson, owner of Geney's Cafe in Halstad.

But for the most part, the town was empty and quiet. Everybody was glued to their radio. The celebrations would have to wait until the bulk of the townspeople and their team returned from Minneapolis.

In South St. Paul, Halstad ran into an even taller opponent than Virginia or Thief River Falls. Prognosticators had to give the bigger team the nod, even though they clearly were pulling for Halstad to stage an upset.

Don Thompson was impressed by South St. Paul. "They're good, all right," Thompson told the *Tribune*, "but height isn't everything. We've been giving away height all year."

South St. Paul coach Ken Fladager was wary of Halstad. He had been planning to play Virginia, and Halstad's dominant first half against the favored Blue Devils gave Fladager the shivers. If there was a sure way to lose one's job as basketball coach at a large school, it was to lose to a tiny hick town from the prairie. Fladager decided to take no chances. He figured his boys would be better off if they slept in their own beds. After hours, Fladager snuck his team out of the Curtis Hotel and sent them home to get a good night's rest.

The game against South St. Paul started well for the Pirates. With another record crowd 85 percent behind them, and with Jimmy Akason leading the charge, Halstad jumped out to a 7–2 lead with its patented fast break. The lead grew to 9–3, and the crowd was delirious. But then South St. Paul gathered its wits and employed its height advantage to out-rebound and out-shoot Halstad in the second quarter.

South St. Paul ran a tight zone defense. Akason pumped in 16 for the Pirates, while center Don Thompson was held to 10 points. The closest Halstad would come, led by charges by Akason, would be 6 points. The Pirates just couldn't get the ball inside.

After the outcome of the game became obvious, Kerrigan put in his entire bench. Young Don Lervold, Bobby Olson, Marlyn Aanenson, and Frankie Steenerson finished the game on the floor. South St. Paul won 61–48. It was far from a blowout, but the game's outcome, in retrospect, wasn't in doubt after the second quarter when South St. Paul figured out how to handle Halstad's fast break.

For Halstad, the loss was but a small disappointment. It was better to lose by a decent margin than to lose on a last-second shot, only to look forward to a lifetime of "what ifs." The townspeople were philosophical. Halstad's shots just didn't drop. The boys had gone farther than anybody had anticipated, and they had provided the entire state with chills and thrills. That was enough. And there was still the third-place consolation game to look forward to.

In 1952, the subdistrict tournament played consolation games down to seventh place. Basketball was so popular that fans demanded to know the pecking order right down to the lowest spot. Halstad wasn't about to let up at all.

Their opponent, perennial state-tournament entry

Austin, the largest school in the state with a graduating class of 350, may have had a tougher time motivating themselves for the third-place game. This was their basketball team's sixteenth trip to the Big Show. Austin never arrived at a tournament without expecting to win, but they had run into a mighty tough Hopkins squad in the semifinal. Hopkins would eventually win the title, the first of three consecutive state titles for Butsie Maetzold's teams. The Austin attack centered on twin brothers, the five-foot-six-inch Rasmussen twins, Don and Dayle, who, according to the *Tribune*, "climb into the opponents' hair at the opening whistle and never get out."

But before Austin and Halstad could tangle on Saturday afternoon, March 22, 1952, they had to get to Williams Arena. Late in the morning, it started to snow. By the time the teams were to leave the Curtis Hotel for the short drive to the arena, over one foot of snow had fallen. It was a full-fledged blizzard. Street cars were derailed, blocking traffic. The Halstad boys had to get out several times to push the three cars to the arena.

There is a myth in Minnesota that the state boys' basketball tournament draws blizzards. However, a look through the weather records shows that the blizzard on March 22, 1952, was the first time a state tournament had been affected by the snow. Since that time, only three or four tournaments have been impacted by storms. The "tournament snowstorm" story is just a myth, and it started in 1952.

The Halstad band was housed in open barracks at the University of Minnesota, just next to Williams Arena. However, on Saturday morning, the band members went uptown to tour around. Some went to a movie. Others visited Halstad people who were fortunate enough to have a hotel room.

Then the snow started. Most of the band was marooned. A dozen or so ended up watching the game on the snowy black and white television in the hotel room of a Halstad resident. Only a handful of the band members made it back to campus to Williams Arena for the game, and those few didn't bother to bring their instruments.

But the game went on, and despite the nearly impossible weather conditions, an estimated 10,000 people saw the beginning of the game. By the end, the arena was nearly full. A blizzard wasn't going to stop fans from seeing the biggest show of the Minnesota winter.

Once again, even though many of the Halstad fans missed the game due to the weather, the crowd that did appear loudly favored Halstad. Austin, after all, was the biggest school in the state, and Halstad, at least a few decades before, had been the smallest town in the state with its own high school. The Pirates were still the darlings.

Unlike the previous four games in tournament play, Halstad came out slowly against Austin. The lead switched several times in the first quarter, with Austin ahead at the end of the period 17–16. Dayle Rasmussen was hot. He would finish with 28 points, while twin brother, Don, would be limited to 3.

Halstad got hot in the second quarter. The old veterans of the 1949 team kicked into gear. Hesby had his best game of the tournaments, eventually scoring 14 points. Thompson was scoring from underneath. And Jimmy Akason, as ever, led the charge. At halftime, Halstad led by nine, 32–23. As the crowd filtered out into the concourse to smoke and check on the blizzard raging outdoors, Halstad appeared to be in control.

Halstad came out red hot in the third period. Don Thompson scored and the Pirates went up by 14 points. However, on the next trip down the court, Thompson came down hard on his ankle, spraining it. Thompson was out, and the Austin team came roaring back.

Thompson had been leading the scoring for Halstad. His absence—the first time he had been off the floor for any length of time during the tournament—hurt the Pirates. As he limped to the locker room, he thought for sure it was the end of his career, but he was in for a surprise. A University of Minnesota trainer who knew his stuff sat the Halstad center up on a table and wrapped enough tape around his ankle to keep it stationary.

"That thing was so tight, it was like I was in a cast," said Thompson.

After tying his Converse All-Stars around the mass of tape, Thompson went back to courtside. By the start of the fourth quarter, Thompson was back in the game, apparently no worse for wear.

In Thompson's absence, Austin rallied from the 14–point deficit to take the lead in the fourth quarter 50–48. Akason helped Halstad score 6 consecutive points to retake a 4-point lead before he fouled out of the game. Austin's hero of the hour, Dayle Rasmussen, scored two quick baskets to tie the game at 54–54 and send it into overtime.

Bernhagen started the overtime with a bucket for Halstad, but Rasmussen answered with two more to put Austin in the lead. Austin then attempted to stall, but traveled. Halstad got the ball in to Thompson, who tied the game up as the first overtime ended.

The second overtime, according to the rules, would be sudden death. The first basket would be the winner. The center jump would be crucial. In the huddle between the overtime periods, Darrel Hesby asked Ray Kerrigan, "What do we do? If I get the ball and have an open shot from outside, do I take it and risk losing the rebound, or do I try to get it in to Thompson for the close shot?" The Pirates had never been in a sudden death situation before.

Kerrigan didn't hesitate. He told Hesby to take the shot.

Thompson, sprained ankle and all, tipped the ball to Bernhagen. Bernhagen passed it to Hesby. Hesby dribbled to the left of the top of the key. It was a long shot but Hesby had never hesitated to take long shots and, given Kerrigan's instructions in the huddle, he didn't hesitate now. The "bespectacled little towhead," as the newspapers called him, put the ball up, and only seven seconds into the second overtime the ball went through the net, giving Halstad third place in the 1952 Minnesota State Tournament. The crowd roared its approval.

Although Hesby took the final winning shot, the most crucial player of the Austin game was Don Thompson. Thompson ended up scoring 20 points. His importance to the Pirates was underscored by their slump when he left the game with a sprained ankle in the third period. When he returned, so did Halstad's scoring touch. Although Jimmy Akason was named to the All-Tournament Team and Thompson was not, many people thought both teammates should have been included. Surprisingly, both Rasmussen twins from Austin were named to the team, even though Dayle's performance in the tournament was far better than Don's. It seemed that the men in the press box didn't think it was fair to honor one identical twin without honoring the other, no matter how different their performances. As a result, Thompson was left out.

Even the newspaper in Thief River Falls was outraged. "In choosing the All-State team, it is hard to understand how they could have left Don Thompson off the team simply because he is not as colorful and such a standout in appearance."

Halstad's basketball season was over. By any stretch of the imagination, their year was a wild success. Third place at the time meant that there were roughly 480 teams in the state who didn't do as well as they did. Not bad for a school with a senior class of twenty-six.

Austin's team left before accepting their trophy. They did so because their bus driver said he was leaving right away, and if the players wanted a ride, they'd better get on the bus now. Their absence at the awards ceremony raised eyebrows, even given the raging blizzard outside. Many fans booed. Newspapers wondered if the Austin coach was pouting over losing to tiny Halstad.

Halstad, on the other hand, stayed to watch Hopkins win the state final. The Pirates accepted their trophy and Jim Akason took his place on the All-State team alongside the state's great players. He had finished his career with 1,640 points and was, although nobody knew it at the time, the Minnesota career leader in that category.

All of Halstad's Starting Five had played critical roles in the success of the Pirates. Dale Serum's scoring bursts had gotten the team through the later qualifying rounds. Morrie Holm, although he didn't rack up many points, was an uncanny rebounder and a pesky defender. Jimmy Akason led the attack on the floor. Darrel Hesby, although relegated to the bench for several quarters, came through against Austin to have his best game in many weeks. It was a sweet victory for Hesby when he got the final basket of the season. His senior year had otherwise been less successful than his previous two.

But overall, it was Don Thompson who was Halstad's most solid and indispensable player in the state tournament. So quietly solid and consistent that he sometimes didn't get noticed, Thompson saved the best basketball in his life for the three games in Williams Arena. He faced down and outscored three taller players. And he came back to the floor in the last game against Austin after sustaining an injury which would have put most players out of the game for good.

Once the tournament ended, Ray Kerrigan was completely shot. He had lost fifteen pounds over the previous month. He had smoked a lot of cigarettes and lost a lot of sleep plotting strategy during the furious month of March Madness. By the next morning, he had fallen ill. It was left to Don Thompson, who by Sunday morning could barely walk due to his swollen ankle, to drive Kerrigan's car through the snow back to Halstad. The nearly 300-mile trip took ten hours.

All of the boys were exhausted, but they showed up to collect their accolades in school on Monday morning. Superintendent Arnold Kittleson reported to the *Fargo Forum* that the mood at school on Monday was subdued, due to the rugged trip home Sunday. As for Ray Kerrigan, he was so sick Monday morning he stayed in bed.

A *Forum* reporter finally found Ray Kerrigan in his home on Tuesday. Assistant Coach Larry Macleod was visiting, as were Kittleson and Erwin Warner. The four discussed the tournament. Kerrigan figured he was ready for a padded cell. Macleod told the reporter that things were "returning to normalcy" in school on Tuesday. And Kittleson maintained that he had to swallow a financial loss on five tickets for the final game against Austin.

The *Minneapolis Tribune* conducted a tournament postmortem. Hopkins had been the favorite, and they came through, as expected. Although the tournament had been exciting, it had gone according to the predictions, except for one thing: Nobody expected Halstad's first-round victory over Virginia. The Pirates also defied expectations by leading the tournament in scoring percentage with 42 percent. Overall, in the tournament, 1,172 shots were taken by the teams, and 446 dropped in the basket. The newspaper figured this percentage of 38 percent was astonishing, certainly the highest ever. The mark was used to argue that the skill level of the players was improving annually.

The tourney was a grand show, columnist Charles Johnson of the *Minneapolis Star* concluded. "It's a good thing it doesn't come oftener than once a year. The nerves couldn't take it."

Over 300 telegrams of congratulations addressed to

the Pirates found their way to the Kerrigan household. Thief River radio station KTRF wired its congratulations. Another message was signed by "blind referee Vic Anderson" of Moorhead, who had worked several Halstad games.

Chambers of Commerce from an eighty-mile radius chimed in with accolades. Most teams in the region sent telegrams, as did many student councils. An especially kind message came in which was signed, simply, "four Waubun senior girls."

As school returned to its normal pace, Clarence Stennes worked up the courage to approach his hero, Jimmy Akason, in the library to autograph his state tournament program. Akason not only agreed to sign but took the program around to several other players and had them sign it as well. It was a gesture that Clarence appreciates to the present day, mentioning it to Akason virtually every time they meet.

The job of honoring the returning heroes was taken on in high style by Rev. Carl and Mrs. Opsahl and the Halstad Lutheran Church. They held a "Youth Recognition Service" three weeks after the team returned from Minneapolis. Five hundred people attended. It was a completely Lutheran affair, although Chuck Bernhagen and Larry Macleod, the only two non-Lutherans affiliated with the team, attended as well.

The service was held in the gym. The Halstad Band played, this time with a full contingent of musicians, including the basketball team. Mrs. Hellerud performed an organ solo, Paul Opsahl a trumpet solo. The Halstad Lutheran choir sang "Remember Now Thy Creator." An octet sang a song entitled "My Task." A trio sang a song entitled "But the Lord is Mindful of His Own."

Rev. Carl Opsahl was the master of ceremonies. Coaches Macleod and Kerrigan spoke as did Superintendent Kittleson. The band director thanked the town for sending the band to Minneapolis. A guest minister from Shelly gave the invocation. Sportscasters and newspapermen gave speeches, including John Pfund, editor of Ada's paper, who said that once his town realized their boys weren't going to defeat the Pirates, they jumped on the Halstad bandwagon. Jimmy Akason spoke for the team, and Janice Stole spoke for the cheerleaders. Rev. L. E. Tallakson, president of the North Dakota District of the Evangelical Lutheran Church, delivered the keynote address, entitled "Pressing Towards the Highest," in which he behooved the players to become "spiritually trim" and press on towards a closer relationship with Jesus Christ.

For all the pomp and circumstance, the most memorable moment of the evening, at least to many of those who recalled the night fifty-odd years later, was when Jake Christianson, famous football coach at Concordia College in Moorhead, stood up to speak.

"He told the filthiest joke," remembered Halstad assistant coach Larry Macleod, shaking his head. "It was just plain risqué."

Other attendees remembered an off-color joke as well, and the discomfort it caused among all present, but nobody seemed to remember the joke itself—except for the minister's son, Paul Opsahl. It went something like this.

A city kid went to the farm. When the farmer took the city kid into the barn, they saw a bunch of piglets nursing at a sow's side. The city kid was intrigued.

"Why are those baby pigs blowing up those little balloons?" he asked.

That was the joke. To paraphrase Paul Opsahl, fifty-some years later, the definition of risqué has certainly changed since 1952.

The long program was followed by a Lutheran lunch of open-faced, egg-salad sandwiches, hot dishes, Jell-O with carrots and celery chunks, and a couple of dozen desserts. Nobody among the 500 went away hungry. And the event was reported prominently in the national Lutheran youth magazine later in the year. The freewill offering taken at the gathering would go towards a new youth room at the church.

Meanwhile, Halstad's newspaper of record, the hapless *Valley Journal*, missed publishing the biggest story in its existence. While preparing the state tournament issue, editor Glenn Smaby, who with his wife formed the entire newspaper staff, poured hot lead on his foot. The injury prevented publication for one week.

The next week, with the help of John Pfund, the publisher of the *Norman County Index* in neighboring Ada, the *Valley Journal* was printed and contained an avalanche of letters sent in by former Halstad residents from around the country who were proud of their team. "It took an Irishman to lead a bunch of Norwegians," said one writer of Ray Kerrigan.

Halstad residents, current and former, were asked their favorite moments. Herman Helleloid, the man who flew in from California, assured the paper that Halstad's performance had been the "thrill of my life."

John Sulerud, who closed Sulerud Hardware to

attend the tournament, said a man from South Dakota had pulled him aside after a game and said, "That Halstad team has the sparkle!"

Another Halstad resident expressed pride in Halstad's high-school girls, declaring that "there was no fainting among them, no hysterics," even after the loss to South St. Paul.

Halstad hardware man Larry Foley, a rabid fan like his business competitor John Sulerud, said the high-light was Hesby's final shot, although Jack Stromberg's late basket in the Virginia final was a thrill as well. "It seemed like an hour before the referee declared the shot no good."

Editor Smaby devoted an entire article in the late edition of the *Valley Journal* to thanking KVOX's Manny Marget for his good broadcasts of the game. "His almost superhuman ability to remember names and use them in big moments with never a recourse to numbers delighted those of us to whom mere numbers would have been confusing," Smaby declared.

Indeed, Marget, who broadcast every game of the tournament, not just those involving Halstad, had gotten over his resentment of Halstad's tournament appearance and turned into a Pirate partisan, even telling stories about the Halstad boys during broadcasts of other games.

Finally, the hometown newspaper speculated on the place the 1952 basketball team's performance would take in Halstad history. "It will live for generations," editor Smaby declared, "just as Joe Schou's immortal triple play."

Editor Smaby's prediction was half correct. The 1952 team is still remembered today, as the picture hanging on the wall in the Halstad Cafe in 2007 clearly shows. But the triple play by the "immortal" Joe Schou is long forgotten.

Chapter 11

Baseball in Halstad

The snow melts slowly on the prairies of northwestern Minnesota. March is a month of false starts with warm days when puddles form followed by cold nights when they freeze to a crisp. The best hope is to get rid of the snow by early April. Even in April you might have a setback—a few days in a row when the temperature doesn't rise above the single digits and perhaps a two-day blizzard for good measure.

As a result, baseball seasons in the north, particularly for high school teams, are short. Early season baseball practices are held indoors and are limited to conditioning and playing catch. As soon as the ground thaws and solidifies enough to support baseball players, practice moves outside. But if you've ever hit the ball on the wrong part of the bat and felt your hands buzz with pain, or caught a line drive right in the palm of the glove instead of in the pocket, you've known a form of excruciating pain that is doubled when you're playing in 38-degree weather.

Baseball as a high school sport in Minnesota had only begun after World War II. The first state high school tournament was held in 1946. But thanks to a thriving town-team baseball tradition, young ballplayers in small towns had many opportunities to hone their skills on the diamond. In fact, thanks to Erwin Warner, Halstad's Mr. Baseball, the high school boys had played more competitive baseball than any other sport. Not only were most of them on Erwin's town team, but they also played on a Jaycee-sponsored team and a team sponsored by the American Legion. Even when one doesn't count the games on the high school schedule, the boys played up to sixty games per summer. And when they weren't playing a game, Erwin Warner conducted practices.

Erwin wasn't just Mr. Baseball. He had his fingers in all Halstad athletics. He never was far from Coach Ray Kerrigan's ear throughout the entire Halstad sports year. Erwin farmed, but everybody knew that sports were his first love—especially baseball.

If it was Ray Kerrigan's job as principal to hire at least one teacher per year who could play ball, Erwin Warner regarded it as his job to provide the ballplayers with jobs, either on his farm or at the Rural Electric Co-op, where one of his friends was the manager.

"He was like a second father to us," said catcher Dale Serum. Serum didn't have much interest in his father's trade of carpentry, so Erwin Warner hired the boy to keep his books on the farm. Erwin's books were in such a mess that a CPA couldn't have figured them out, much less a seventeen-year-old high-school kid, but keeping good books wasn't the point. Giving a job to a kid who needed one was what was important.

After the war, it was Erwin who brought town baseball back to life in Halstad. And when it became apparent in the early 1950s that a lot more money could be made if the local baseball field had lights, Erwin led the charge. When doubting Toms wondered who would change the bulbs, Erwin said "I'll climb up there and change 'em myself."

The prospect of chubby Erwin Warner, just over five feet tall, climbing those sixty-foot poles might well have sold enough tickets to pay for the entire project.

Erwin farmed across the river in North Dakota, but baseball was always his priority. It could be the middle of harvest, but when the hour of 4 o'clock hit, everything shut down and Erwin Warner and the ballplayers who worked for him would rush back to town, either for a game or for practice. If they were playing far away, they might leave the farm at noon.

Erwin put up one of the first batting cages ever

seen in the area in the backyard of his house in town. He bought equipment for the team. He drove the players to countless games, some over 100 miles distant, in one of his rickety cars. After the game, he might treat the team to a steak dinner, a practice he frequently extended to Halstad basketball players during the winter. "We ate more steak dinners off of Erv than anybody," according to Dale Serum.

When Serum decided to head west to play ball in California with Rod Oistad, the best pitcher Halstad ever had, Erwin Warner gave them a car and told the two to sell it in California for spending money. When Serum lived in Alexandria, Minnesota, in later years, and Erwin needed him to come back to Halstad to catch a game for the old town team, Erwin hired a pilot and a Piper Cub to make the 160-mile trip to Alexandria. Serum was flown in for the game and delivered back to Alexandria afterwards.

Erwin's interest in kids wasn't limited to baseball. He put at least one of the town's kids through college when it became apparent the boy couldn't make it on his own.

"He was gruff," one former player said, "but you knew he really cared."

Always on the lookout for good ballplayers from area towns, Erwin was known to offer the parents of a high school prospect jobs in Halstad if they would move. Although the only documented recruit to the high school teams to Erwin's credit was the relocation of his nephew Chuck Bernhagen to Halstad for his senior year in 1951–52, Erwin brought in many baseball players for the summer to play on the town team. This often involved finding various shady ways to compensate them while staying within division rules that prohibited paying the players.

Even as an old man, Erwin continued his devotion to Halstad athletics. After his son Cactus took over the basketball coaching duties at Halstad in the late 1970s, Erwin offered the late Ray Kerrigan's daughter room, board, and a job in Halstad if she would move there with her talented son Chad. Chad stayed in Moorhead, where he started on a team that won the Minnesota state title in 1988.

For his efforts on behalf of Halstad athletics, Erwin was lauded by the town fathers. In the early 1950s, they held a ceremony and presented Erwin with an expensive engraved watch. But for all he was loved and respected by his players, and for all he did for the community of Halstad, and for all of his friends in the baseball world, Erwin Warner was no saint.

Blackballed from the saloons in Halstad as a young

man due to his propensity to get drunk and start fights, Erwin Warner was left to drive to neighboring towns to get drunk and start fights. When the Norman County Fair was in neighboring Ada, Erwin and some of his rough buddies would get drunk, go to the fair, and look for a rumble.

When Erwin married Madelyn Hesby in 1939, he calmed down a little, but not much. For the most part, after his marriage, he took out his aggressions on umpires and opposing players. But occasionally, things would boil over and Erwin would get into a brawl.

Each year, he took the Halstad team nearly 200 miles north to Warroad, Minnesota, for a tournament. One year, they stopped at the Legion in Warroad for a few drinks on the way out of town. A Warroad bar patron seemed to think Darrel Hesby had insulted him. He wanted to take it outside.

Halstad player-coach Joe Oistad tried to mediate the dispute. He urged the team up the stairs from the basement bar and got them out the door. Once in the alley out back, the dispute calmed down into a bunch of snorting and pawing at the dirt. Oistad thought he had things under control.

But Erwin couldn't stand it. He walked up to the

bar patron and punched him in the face. Blood spewed everywhere. The tangling two crashed into some nearby scaffolding which fell with a clang. Chaos broke loose.

Erwin was not only short and fat, but at the time of the trip to Warroad, he was for some long-forgotten reason encased in a body cast. He and the bar patron rolled on the ground, pounding on each other. Those present have one outstanding memory: the hollow "thump thump" of fists banging on Erwins's body cast.

Eventually, voice-of-reason Joe Oistad managed to get everybody in their cars and headed back on the long trip to Halstad. When some players jumped in the back seat of one car, there was Hesby, down on the floor hiding. Down the road a ways, Erwin realized that the engraved watch given him by the community fathers was gone. It had fallen off in the alley behind the bar. A Warroad player dropped the watch off in Halstad a few days later.

Erwin's reputation as a prominent member of the community did much to cover up his many foibles. The conservative Lutherans seemed to have no problem entrusting their sons to Erwin's care, despite his reputation for profanity and off-color jokes.

"He was like one of us," says one former player of Erwin. "He'd joke with you about sleeping with the neighbor's daughter."

"That's not the type of stuff you got at home, that's for sure," the player recalls with a snicker. "So, we liked Erwin."

Speedy center-fielder Wally Oien remembers returning to the dugout after getting caught stealing. Erwin Warner wasn't happy. "Jesus Christ, Wally, did you put the plow down?" he snarled in his nasal tone.

Erwin once scheduled a game in Bagley, eighty miles to the east. As the team arrived in three jam-packed cars, it started to rain. The game was canceled. Erv decided that they should go on to Duluth, 160 miles farther down the road, to watch the Duluth-Superior minor-league team play. As they arrived at that ballpark, it started to rain again. The game in Duluth was canceled. So, the three carloads of ballplayers went to the Duluth zoo before heading back all the way across the state of Minnesota to Halstad. During the all-night drive, one of the cars went off the road when the driver, a ballplayer, fell asleep. Luckily, he was aimed down a side road and woke up before flipping the car into the ditch.

"When we got home," says Wally Oien, many years later, "the roosters were crowing, and so was my mother."

The scheduling of town team baseball games was a loose affair where the area's coaches got together at a neutral site with a good watering hole and drew up the calendar with the assistance of copious amounts of beer. The results of the meetings sometimes confused even the participants.

Erwin once led the three-car caravan north to Red Lake Falls to play their local team in their cozy, little ballpark along the Red Lake River. When they got to Red Lake (which is short for Red Lake Falls in the local parlance, even though there is another town by the name of Red Lake only a few miles to the east), the ballpark was empty. No players, no fans. Erwin ran up town and found one of the Red Lake Falls players.

"No, we have no game scheduled tonight."

"Yes you do," Erwin replied.

"Well," the player said, "maybe our coach was drinking too much at the meeting and wrote it down wrong." The player rounded up the coach, the team, and a little crowd, and they started a game.

About the third inning, a winded Red Lake Falls resident came down to the ballpark to find Erwin Warner.

"They're calling from Devils Lake," the man said.

"They have a grandstand full of 2,500 people, a team on the field, and they are wondering where you are."

Turns out it was Erwin Warner who had been drinking too much at the coaches' meeting. He mixed up Red Lake with Devils Lake, North Dakota, a city out about 115 miles to the west. After finishing the game in Red Lake Falls, Erwin found a phone and called Devils Lake to clear up the mess. The next night, Erwin and the boys headed west in the three-car caravan for a make-up game in Devils Lake.

Erwin Warner loved baseball and his players loved him so much that after he died in 1995, Erwin's players from over the years, with the help of Larry Macleod, set up a scholarship fund in his memory.

But, in the words of Dale Serum, "I think Erwin's baseball got in the way of his farming."

To say the least.

Erwin Warner's farming operation was slipshod at best, comic at worst. Erwin hired any ballplayer who needed a job to work on the farm. There was rarely enough for them all to do, so they sometimes practiced baseball on company time. They were free to fill the gas tanks on their cars from the farm tank. Erwin retained other employees as well, rough types who frequently showed up with hangovers if they showed up at all. With no evident cap on labor expenses, Erwin Warner's farming operation was always hanging by its financial fingernails.

When he needed cash, Erwin would load up a big sow in the back seat of his car and bring it to town to sell. One Halstad resident remembers meeting Erwin's old car on the road. Because Erwin was too short to see over the steering wheel, all you could see was the pig's head where the driver's head should be. It looked for all the world like a pig was driving the car.

Later in life, an incident occurred which was a metaphor for Erwin Warner's farming career. He reached up into the cab of a tractor to turn it on. The big tractor started, but it was in gear and ran over Erwin, who was standing in front of the dual tires. After flattening Erwin, the tractor ran into a gas tank, which blew up and burned down the machine shed.

Luckily for Erwin, the ground was wet and soft. Just as luckily, the tractor's weight was spread out between the two big tires. Erwin Warner lived, but not without another several weeks spent in a body cast.

Erwin Warner's bills accumulated. He owed money all over town. In fact, one bulk oil dealer lost his job largely because he had extended Erwin Warner five digits of credit, and Erwin never paid it back.

So, a large portion of those steak dinners, plane trips, donated cars, tuition checks, the gas—so many of the wonderful things Erwin Warner did for the athletes of Halstad, were done with money which wasn't really his. But to hear the residents of Halstad tell it today, Erwin Warner, even in the words of those he stiffed to the tune of thousands of dollars, was a wonderful and generous man. Such is life in the small town. Over the decades, you are exposed to both the good and bad of your neighbors. In the end—at the funeral if theirs comes first—it's usually best just to laugh off the bad. After all, they'd have done the same thing for you.

Town amateur baseball exploded in popularity following World War II, quickly reaching its peak in Minnesota in 1950 when approximately 800 teams took the field around the state. Some towns supported as many as three teams. There were two divisions. Division A was for teams that brought in some semiprofessional players, and Division B was for teams which were, on paper at least, completely amateur. However, the rules were open to various interpretations, and the definition of the word "amateur" was often stretched to the breaking point. Players were briefed on the details of their phantom jobs, for which they were being well-paid, in the minutes before they took the field for their new team—just in case some snooping officials happened to show up. Many of the jobs given players were slightly more legitimate, requiring players to at least show up at the phone company or the implement dealership every now and then, whether they did a lick of work or not.

Southern Minnesota was a town-team hotbed. Town teams competed successfully with minor-league teams for players. Signing of free agents made headlines in the daily sports pages. Future Yankee Moose Skowron cut his teeth with the Austin, Minnesota, team in the early 1950s, to name but one future major-league star who got his start on the ball diamonds of small-town Minnesota.

The rules of the day were a tangled mess, and they changed every year. Organizers tried, unsuccessfully, to prevent players from moving from team to team several times during the season. Disqualifications were common and loudly protested. Teams which didn't win early in the season sometimes folded midseason when it became apparent that they weren't going to sell enough tickets to pay the players.

The games were rough-and-tumble affairs. If fights didn't break out on the field, they might break out in the stands or up at the local watering hole after the game was over. Players taunted their opponents and the umpires mercilessly. Spectators had free reign to abuse the umpires as they saw fit. Sportsmanship was unheard of. Baseball in the 1950s was anything but a dignified affair.

Needless to say, Erwin Warner fit right in. As founder and manager of Halstad's Red Sox, he was the godfather of Halstad baseball. At little more than five-foot-one-inch, Erwin was out-shorted by only one manager in the area, Shorty Dekko of Gary. When Halstad played Gary, the insults would fly.

"Why you standing in a hole, Shorty?" Erwin would yell.

"Get off your knees, Warner, prayin' won't do you no good," Dekko would retort.

The line between good-natured teasing and punch-provoking insults was thin, but most of the time good humor prevailed. When Erwin walked to the mound with his little steps, opposing fans would chant "hup, hup, hup," and Erwin, just to throw them off, would throw in a stutter-step.

From the farmland north of Halstad came one of Minnesota's great town-team pitchers, Rod Oistad. Oistad eventually helped pitch the Minnesota Gophers to a national NCAA title in 1956, but in the years before, he was Erwin Warner's ace. Oistad could throw in the lower 90s, and he had a curve that broke nearly two feet. He was wild enough to provoke fear but tame enough to throw several no-hitters in his career.

Rod Oistad graduated from Halstad in 1951, so he wasn't on the successful 1952 teams. But he played both baseball and basketball beside the Starting Five and the others in 1950 and '51.

Erwin Warner scheduled his town team to play some good talent around the area in the late 1940s, but Halstad didn't fare too well at first. In the 1949 season, they lost to the Mayville Redcats, a perennial North Dakota power, by a football-like score.

"Then, Rod came," according to Jimmy Akason, who was the town team's shortstop almost from the time he entered high school, "and he could throw the ball."

The next time the two teams played, Oistad shut down Mayville and Halstad scored an upset. Just as the victory over Thief River Falls in basketball in 1949 awoke the players to their potential, so too, that victory over Mayville made Halstad's young baseball players realize that they had something going.

With Erwin at the helm and Oistad on the mound, Halstad became a town-team powerhouse in northern

Minnesota. Oistad would come and go during his college years and after, but he was in town enough to help Erwin Warner put Halstad's baseball team on the map.

As with basketball, the main baseball rivalry for Halstad was with Ada. Again, to quote Ada's Dick Nielson, "There was no love."

After defeating Ada in one game, Rod Oistad was taking his spikes off before getting in his car. Two men approached him from across the field. Oistad could tell that their intent wasn't good, so he stood. The bigger man said, "You're a bastard!" and took a swing at Oistad. He missed. Oistad took a swing at the man. He connected. Blood flew everywhere.

The shorter man said, "I think that's all he has to say," and the two left.

Fifteen years later, Oistad was pulled aside by a man in Gary, Minnesota.

"You remember me?" he said. Oistad had no idea who he was. "Thanks to you, I drank soup out of a straw for nine months."

It was the man who Oistad had punched. The man apologized.

Another time, Oistad hit a batter whose elbow was

hanging out in the strike zone. His manager argued the play and was thrown out of the game. When the same batter came up two innings later, Oistad's manager jumped the outfield fence and ran to the mound.

"Hit this guy or you'll never pitch for me again."

Oistad didn't want to throw at the guy. The batter was about 5 foot 1 inches tall and couldn't buy a hit. Why not pitch to him and get him out?

The manager, who by now was being dragged off the field by the umpires for the second time in one game, yelled back at Oistad as he departed, "Throw at him, or you're done!"

Oistad plunked the batter on the ribs. A brawl nearly broke out. And when play resumed, the local fans took to throwing golf balls at Oistad while he was on the mound.

Town baseball was rough. In the bigger towns, it was a game for men in their twenties, thirties, and even forties. They chewed tobacco, swore, and drank beer after the game. In Halstad, however, the town was so small and the young crop of athletes was so good that some of the boys were starting on the town team by ninth grade.

Darrel Hesby was small, but fast. He could connect with the ball and drive it or he could bunt and beat out the throw to first. Hesby was an ideal leadoff hitter.

Hesby's ability to infuriate opponents carried over from the basketball court to the ball diamond. In particular, Hesby became known for a play that he allegedly learned from Larry Macleod.

Hesby would lead off the game with a bunt, which he inevitably would beat out. The next batter would be Macleod, who would square up to bunt as well. When he laid the bunt down, the defense would scramble to get Macleod out at first on the sacrifice. Sometimes, but not always, they would succeed. But while the attention was on the play at first, which Macleod's speed always made close, Hesby would run from first to third, cutting second base and crossing right behind the pitcher's mound. Because there were only one or two umpires for each game, Hesby never once got caught. The other team would start the game in a tizzy, arguing violently and vainly, pointing out Hesby's footprints behind the pitcher's mound in the freshly groomed infield dirt, to no avail. Hesby continued to use the play well into his thirties when he played town ball in southern Minnesota.

On the cheating scale, Hesby's cutting second base was seen as a little overboard, even by his own teammates. Erwin Warner surely didn't mind, but others were embarrassed. And when it was Darrel Hesby who was doing the cutting, it was even worse, at least to the other team.

Dale Serum was the catcher from ninth grade on. When he started, he was so small and his arm was so weak that he couldn't throw to second base. If the runner would steal, according to Rod Oistad, Serum would throw the ball back to Oistad on the mound, and Oistad would relay the ball to second base.

"We didn't get too many runners that way," Oistad says today.

However, things changed when Serum started his growth spurt. By the time he was a junior, his arm was the best in the area. From his senior year on, Serum was feared. He could throw out runners from the crouch position. He would pick them off first or third or get them stealing second.

With age, Serum developed the attitude of a typical, grizzled catcher: cranky, take-charge, and no-nonsense. When a pitcher got wild, Serum would fling the ball back to the mound with such authority that it hurt. Combined with his ample ears, Serum's catching abilities earned him the nickname "Yogi" after the premier catcher of the era, the Yankee's Yogi Berra.

Jimmy Akason was going to be a good athlete wherever he played. The marquee position in the field on small-town teams is shortstop. It was a natural spot for the small-town hero to settle.

Behind Oistad in the starting rotation was his cousin Morrie Holm. Although one year older than Oistad, Holm's delayed start in school put him in the class of 1952, one year behind his younger cousin. Holm's maturity—he was nineteen during his senior year—helped out on the basketball floor, where he was steady and dependable, and it helped on the pitcher's mound, where he was unflappable. Although Morrie Holm didn't have Rod Oistad's blazing fastball and roundhouse curve, he was no slouch. He threw from different angles.

"He threw the darndest junk," according to former teammate Wally Oien, who said that he'd rather face Oistad than his cousin Morrie Holm any day of the week. "At least with Rod, you knew what was coming," Oien said.

Ray Kerrigan claimed that Holm could make the ball curve two different directions on one pitch.

Holm had good control, and when Oistad lost his feel for the plate, which happened frequently, Erwin would bring in Holm to get out the side.

At first base for the Halstad team was willowy Marlyn Aanenson. Although Aanenson had slipped into the second tier of the basketball roster late in his career after showing promise as a sophomore, he was always a good first baseman. It was Aanenson's sure glove that allowed Serum to fire the ball to first base with confidence that the ball wouldn't end up going down the right field line. Not a power hitter, Aanenson was a sensible batter, drawing walks and hitting the occasional single.

Several underclassmen in 1952 would also become baseball stars. Curt Johnson started at second base. He would be good enough to go on to play ball in college. Wally Oien was the fastest player on the team, faster even than Macleod and Hesby, and he could play a mean center field. Once he filled out his frame, he showed some pop at the plate as well, once hitting three home runs in a single game. Oien played ball well into his thirties.

Of course, the town team roster wasn't limited to high schoolers. Assistant basketball coach Larry Macleod played in the outfield and batted second. He could bunt, hit for power, and fly like the wind. Another teacher, Bob Dalen, often took the mound. Dalen seemed to do better the more he complained of a sore arm or bad back. And when Chuck Bernhagen arrived from Bird Island for his senior year, not only did he fill out the basketball roster with another capable body, but he could pitch, and Halstad's 1952 high school team, deprived of Rod Oistad by graduation, would need him on the mound.

High school baseball, which had only started after the war, was small peanuts compared to Minnesota high school basketball. Neither could high school baseball hold a candle to town amateur baseball. The crowds were small, the headlines in the newspaper even smaller. But high school baseball was a growing concern, and Ray Kerrigan and Erwin Warner weren't about to miss another chance for their talented boys to play ball. Ray Kerrigan was the coach for the high school team due to his credentials as a teacher, but it was Erwin Warner who taught the boys what they knew, Erwin Warner who helped drive them to every high school baseball game in his old car, and Erwin Warner who was Ray Kerrigan's closest advisor. Thanks to Erwin Warner, the Halstad high school boys had played more baseball against better competition than most of their counterparts in the state. When the snow finally melted in late April of 1952, they were ready to take the field.

Halstad had made its presence known in high school baseball circles as early as 1950, when it made the first appearance by a Halstad team in the state tournament, held that year in Detroit Lakes, only seventy-seven miles away. But Halstad's appearance was a disappointment. Rod Oistad had a 103-degree fever. The Pirates lost two games, one 10–0 and the other 15–0, and were eliminated in the one season where the state tournament was in their own backyard.

In 1951, the team played well. With Oistad as the number one starter and Holm as number two, the team looked to be going to the state tournament again. In the region semifinal, Kerrigan decided to use Rod Oistad against a feared Bemidji team. Before the game, Oistad was going through his routine, which included taking a little nap with his feet up in the dugout. A ball got away from the players warming up in front of the dugout and struck Oistad in a particularly delicate spot. Oistad was so curled up and in pain that Erwin Warner took him uptown for some crackers and tea, for whatever that was worth. The combination worked. Oistad recovered in time to take the mound. As he tells it today, "the game went fine." The box score shows that the game went better than fine. Oistad threw a no-hitter and struck out seventeen Bemidji batters. They didn't so much as hit a fair ball off Oistad. Halstad scored ten runs early and never looked back.

However, in the 1951 region final, the Halstad Pirates ran into an Alvarado team that had saved its best pitcher for the championship game. While he shut Halstad down, Morrie Holm was touched for a couple of runs which were enough to send Halstad home with another disappointing finish to their season. Halstad fans wondered if Ray Kerrigan shouldn't have pulled Rod Oistad from the Bemidji game, no-hitter or not, and saved him for the championship, once the Pirates opened up the big lead. Halstad fans felt they had a better overall team than Alvarado, but pitching wins, and Alvarado had saved their ace for when it mattered.

Even though Rod Oistad wasn't on the high school baseball team the next season, the presence of the pitching star on the town team and the high school team the previous years upped the level of play and sense of excitement which surrounded baseball in Halstad. When the next spring rolled around, the boys who headed out to the diamond after the thaw not only had a recent confidence-building experience at Williams Arena under their belt, but they had every reason to think they could make a mark on the baseball field.

The snowdrifts left late in 1952, and the baseball season couldn't begin until late April. The Halstad Pirates managed to squeeze in only four regular season games before the tournaments started.

None of the games was even close. Halstad began the season by scoring 40 runs against Borup in an incredibly sloppy affair. Wally Oien pitched for the Pirates.

Halstad then defeated the Arthur, North Dakota, team 20–0. Chuck Bernhagen pitched and struck out 14 batters over seven innings. An 8–0 defeat of Ada followed, with Morrie Holm striking out 11 batters.

The subdistrict tournament began against Waubun in mid-May. Chuck Bernhagen struck out 10 of the Bombers and gave up only two hits in seven innings. The Pirates won 18–0. In the subdistrict final, Halstad dispatched Ada 10–2. Morrie Holm struck out ten. The Pirates won the subdistrict title without a hint of opposition.

The district tournaments were next, but the schedule was moving along at a stately pace. The subdistrict final against Ada was played May 21, 1952. The first round of the district tournaments would not be played for three more weeks, on June 10.

During those three weeks, the lilacs bloomed and faded. School closed. The seniors, including Akason, Hesby, Thompson, Holm, Serum, and Bernhagen, graduated and took their senior class trip to Yellowstone Park. Spring turned to summer. The wheat fields and beet fields went from black to green. The trees put on leaves.

In northern Minnesota, more happens in the three weeks from May 21 to June 10 than in any other three-week period during the year. The rhythm of life loses the structure given it by school activities. Country kids lose touch with their school friends and take on summertime friends—usually neighbor kids, visiting cousins, or whoever is available. Older kids work in the fields. Whether the long days on the tractor are blissfully idyllic or unbearably lonely depends upon one's disposition. If you aren't old enough to drive or don't have a car, you are forced to entertain yourself on the farm.

The Halstad Pirate baseball players played ball during their three-week hiatus—Erwin Warner made sure of that. The Halstad Red Sox had started their season, and when they weren't playing, Erwin held practice.

But there was none of the build-up for the high-school baseball tournaments that there had been for the high-school basketball tournaments three months earlier. High-school baseball wasn't even the most important baseball played in Halstad in 1952. Plus, people had other things to do. The weather was beautiful. The urgent fury of March Madness on the basketball floor stems in part from the eagerness of the fans to get out of the house after the long winter months. March is a time of general madness in the north. People have cabin fever. Farmers are desperate to get in the fields, but they know it will be another six weeks before they can turn a wheel. Farm wives are eager to get in the garden, but the snowdrifts five feet deep still bury the plot in the back corner of the yard.

By mid-June, however, people are outside working in the long summer sunshine. The sun sets at about 9:30 p.m. on June 21 at Halstad's latitude and rises again just before 5 a.m. There is lots of work to be done and lots of time in which to do it. Sitting inside on a dark evening and dreaming of glory for your high-school baseball team just isn't on the agenda. You're more likely to be out mending fences until sunset.

Halstad faced Bagley in the first round of district tournament play on Bagley's home field. The Flyers gave the Pirates their first serious competition of the season. Morrie Holm survived a rocky third inning. The Pirates scored 2 in the first, 2 in the third, and never trailed. Morrie struck out eleven. Halstad won 5–3.

Ray Kerrigan enjoyed keeping statistics. The batting statistics for his Pirates, thanks to the short season and the blowout victories over inferior competition, were pretty inflated. Marlyn Aanenson was batting .600. Four other players were batting more than .400. Only Squirt

Johnson was having trouble getting hits. He had one hit all season in seventeen at bats. Johnson's .059 batting average didn't prevent Kerrigan from batting him leadoff in the Bagley game. Johnson came through in the fifth inning, reaching base by getting hit by a pitch.

After Morrie beat Bagley, it would have seemed right for Chuck Bernhagen to take the mound in the district final game against Fosston two days later. But Bernhagen was nowhere to be found. His prickly personality had gotten the best of him. Somewhere in the three weeks off, Bernhagen had talked back to assistant coach Larry Macleod. Kerrigan backed Macleod, of course, and benched Bernhagen. It was going to be up to Bernhagen to come forward to apologize.

Meanwhile, since Halstad had only two reliable starting pitchers and Bernhagen wasn't available, Morrie would have to pitch against Fosston on only one day of rest. He shut down Fosston through the first five innings, but tired in the sixth, giving up five runs. By that time, however, the Pirates had scored 16 runs themselves. Morrie finished the game and the Pirates cruised to a 20–5 victory. Halstad was the champion of District 30.

Before the Region 8 tournament, Erwin Warner convinced his young relative Chuck Bernhagen to apologize to Kerrigan and Macleod. Bernhagen was back, but he had a sore arm. The regional would be played on two consecutive days. This time, Morrie would have to pitch on no days of rest.

Luckily, the first game was yet another blowout, this one over Hallock. When Halstad put up 6 runs in the second inning, it was all but in the bag. Kerrigan decided that this year he would save his ace. In the fourth inning, Kerrigan put in Wally Oien to pitch, even though Morrie hadn't yet given up a hit. Oien put up good numbers for two innings before Kerrigan decided to try Bernhagen for a couple of innings. Sore arm and all, Bernhagen finished off the Hallock nine, giving up only one walk in two innings.

The Region 8 final, played in Bagley on June 19th, pitted Halstad against Cass Lake. Morrie started. Halstad scored early and often. Morrie mowed down the Cass Lake nine, giving up single runs in the third and fourth innings. By then, Halstad had the game well in hand. For the second straight day, Bernhagen came in to mop up. Halstad won the Region 8 title and had qualified for the state tournament by beating Cass Lake 12–2. They had dominated every team they played in their short season except for Bagley in the district tournament, a game they won by 5–3.

But their impressive record did nothing to put the Halstad Pirates on the statewide radar. After all, only two years previously they had been eliminated from the state tournament by a cumulative score of 25–0. Region 8 was regarded as a weak baseball region. In the pretournament prognostications, of the eight teams to appear at the state tournament, only Halstad was never mentioned as having a whisper of a chance to win the title.

With such easy victories, with most fans busy with summer activities, and since Halstad had gone to the state baseball tournament only two years previously, there was none of the euphoria that had accompanied the victory over Thief River Falls in basketball. Arnold Kittleson didn't have to distribute tickets. Nobody flew in from California to watch the home team. In fact, Halstad had entered the state tournament by flying completely under the radar.

Chapter 12

But We Had Morrie

The 1952 state baseball tournament would be held at Dartt's Park in Owatonna, Minnesota. The outstate location would limit the media hoopla. The Twin Cities newspapers were present, but not in crushing numbers. In fact, the Minnesota state baseball tournament was, compared to the Minnesota state basketball tournament, idyllic and peaceful. Dartt's was a beautiful little park, used for the Owatonna town team as well as for Class A minor league baseball. Downtown Owatonna charmed the Halstad players. The hotel was more than adequate, and the townspeople bent over backwards to make sure that they left a favorable impression on the young visitors and their fans.

Each of the eight teams entering the tournament was assigned a sponsor by the Owatonna Chamber of Commerce. That sponsor was to act as host and make sure that the team knew where to go, where to eat, and what to see around town. The Halstad Pirates were assigned the local sheriff. Although he was polite enough, the sheriff, a big, round, jovial man, could barely conceal his disappointment at not being assigned to a team with a fighting chance of winning the tournament.

The Halstad Pirates came into the tournament with two strikes against them. Region VIII didn't have a good baseball reputation. It was far removed from the baseball hotbeds of central and southern Minnesota. The previous Region VIII entries had performed abysmally at the tournament, including Halstad itself two years earlier. There was no reason for the press to give Halstad any advance billing, and they did not. The team's arrival in Owatonna was noted in the newspapers, but that was it.

Halstad wasn't even the smallest town entered in the tournament. That distinction went to Bricelyn, a little town south of the Twin Cities near Faribault. If anybody was the tournament sweetheart, it was Bricelyn with its highly-touted pitcher, Paul Anderson. Paul had allowed only one run in 81 innings throughout the season.

Ray Kerrigan, Arnold Kittleson, and Bake Johnson drove the team down in their cars. Erwin Warner would arrive a little later. Assistant coach Larry Macleod, who had been married four days earlier, would miss the entire tournament due to his honeymoon.

The team practiced on Dartt's Field. The mood was light—so light, in fact, that Arnold Kittleson broke his usual decorum and lit up a cigar. The players, particularly the seniors, were in a boisterous mood. They weren't in school, so Kerrigan and Kittleson didn't hold as much power over them. When Darrel Hesby busted his favorite bat in batting practice, he didn't feel at all restrained. He let loose with some profanity worthy of a boy who, as the proud owner of a high school diploma, was now a full adult.

Kittleson overheard. He lit into Hesby in no uncertain terms.

"You are representing Halstad," he said, "you are not to curse." No more cigars for Arnold Kittleson, either. Propriety returned to the proceedings.

The Pirates then attended the opening banquet Tuesday evening. Colorful sportscaster Halsey Hall spoke, as did Owatonna's mayor and a handful of other dignitaries. The only dark cloud over the proceedings was the weather. Rain was predicted for the entire three-day affair.

On Wednesday, the games began. In the third game of the day, Halstad played New Ulm under the lights, starting at 9 p.m. Morrie Holm, Halstad's ace, was in good form, but so was New Ulm's ace, Rollie Schaper. Each pitcher gave up only three hits. The difference, as is so often the case in high school games, came in the fielding department. New Ulm committed six errors to Halstad's five, but New Ulm's miscues came at more crucial times.

Darrel Hesby started out the game with a bunt down the third base line, as was his custom. He beat out the play for an infield hit. Chuck Bernhagen, starting in left field, then hit a ground ball that was mishandled. Both runners were safe, and as New Ulm struggled to prevent them from advancing further, two wild throws allowed both Hesby and Bernhagen to score. In the second inning, Marlyn Aanenson walked and eventually scored on a wild pitch, giving the Pirates a 3–0 lead.

On the mound, Morrie cruised. He struck out the first five batters he faced. He gave up two hits through the first six innings and only walked two batters the entire game. Although his defense softened in the seventh and final inning, allowing New Ulm to score 3 runs, 2 of them unearned, Morrie was spectacular. He struck out fourteen batters in seven innings.

The sheriff, like broadcaster Manny Marget three months earlier during the state basketball tournament, was having a change of heart. He could see that the Halstad boys could play. He became friendlier, and the boys took to him in return.

The next opponent was St. Louis Park. Ray Kerrigan

was in a bind, but so are most high school coaches in short tournaments. Where are you going to find pitchers enough for three consecutive games? Bernhagen would start the game, but his arm was sore. Halstad now was assured of two more games no matter what happened. Who was going to pitch? Halstad's third pitcher was Wally Oien, the regular center fielder. He had one start during the season and did reasonably well, but that was against inferior competition. Putting Oien in to pitch would be a last resort, something Kerrigan would do only when Halstad had been all but eliminated. Shortstop Jimmy Akason had once pitched, but he was a stop-gap solution.

The man of the moment was Morrie Holm. Morrie would be on deck in case Bernhagen couldn't do the job. If Halstad lost, Morrie might be able to give them a few innings in the final game before Kerrigan turned it over to the scrubs.

Morrie Holm was a country kid through and through. Raised seven miles northeast of Halstad on a small farm near the Marsh River, he was the tenth of eleven children. His father, Palmer Holm, a quiet Norwegian farmer, struggled to eke out enough of a living to support his enormous family. However, Palmer wasn't entirely preoccupied with work. He had been a pitcher himself, way back when they had township teams. Palmer and his brothers were known as good ballplayers back when they used cow pies for bases.

When Morrie went to town to school in fourth grade, he was painfully shy. As a country kid, he was subject to the usual taunts from the town kids. He remembers winning a foot race in elementary school, only to overhear the other kids express surprise that a "dumb farm kid" could run so fast.

When he was at home, Morrie threw anything he could get his hands on. He threw rocks at fence posts, rocks at the power poles, baseballs at the barn, apples, whatever he could pick up. He developed pinpoint control.

Morrie's first cousin Rodney Oistad lived nearby. The two frequently played catch. Neighbor Marlyn Aanenson sometimes joined them. Rodney could throw harder than Morrie, but Morrie could throw at any angle and always seemed to have stuff on the ball. Rodney's older brother Joe knew a thing or two about pitching, and he gave Morrie the only coaching Morrie ever had on pitches, form, and strategy. Sometimes they would harrow a patch of ground and hold a game. Participants would be completely covered in black dust by the end. "Boy, did we have fun," Morrie recalls today.

Morrie's teammates remember him as a junk ball

pitcher. However, they inevitably compare him to his cousin Rod. Yes, Morrie wasn't as fast as Rod Oistad, but Rod's arm was the best around. Professional scouts and college coaches eventually estimated that Rod Oistad threw in the lower 90s. Opponents who batted against Morrie but not Rod claim that Morrie threw plenty hard, probably at least in the mid-80s. And his ability to mix up arm angles and grips made him seem, to some, more confusing to bat against than Rod.

Morrie was a deliberate worker on the mound. Although he seldom walked batters, he didn't mind running up a full count. Between pitches, he walked behind the mound, played with the rosin bag, and generally irritated anybody who might want to get home before supper. At the state tournament, a broadcaster allowed his annoyance with Morrie to show:

"There he goes with those rituals again," he said, without noting that, although it was taking awhile, Morrie was eventually getting the batters out.

Before the state tournament, Morrie had some successes on the mound, both with the high school team and with the town team. Although he had operated in the shadow of his cousin Rod Oistad, Morrie was at least known around Halstad as a reliable #2 starter. However, his renown had not spread. Nobody down south knew about Morrie Holm when the state tournament started. They would soon.

Against St. Louis Park, Bernhagen made it through one inning. After throwing a few pitches in the second inning, he threw in the towel. His arm hurt too badly. Morrie was eager for the ball, so Kerrigan gave it to him, despite his complete game the previous day.

Again, Halstad got off to a fast start. Again, the Pirates were the beneficiary of an opponent's sloppy fielding. Two errors in the first inning, combined with hits by Morrie and Marlyn Aanenson and a walk to Jimmy Akason, led Halstad to a 4–0 first-inning lead. The Pirates added 3 more in the second inning thanks to three more St. Louis Park errors, and that would be all the runs the Halstad side needed. Morrie finished the game, stifling the potent St. Louis Park offense. He gave up 6 hits and two walks, but he struck out eight and was awarded with his second win in two days.

Now the sheriff was a big fan. He cheered Halstad loudly. He proclaimed that they were going to win the state title.

Halstad had reached the state final. The championship game would be a rematch, of sorts. The other bracket produced the Austin Packers as its finalist. Once again, three months after they beat Austin for the third-place trophy at Williams Arena, Halstad would see the Rasmussen twins and some other familiar faces from the largest school in the state.

Finally, the media started to pay attention to Halstad. As if to make up for lost time, the *Owatonna Daily People's Press* published an article on Halstad's mayor, who noted that one-tenth of the town's population, 50 people, had driven to Owatonna for the tournament; another article on Ray Kerrigan, who gave Erwin Warner credit for training the boys in baseball's basics; and a third article on the farm boys from Halstad who were "cottoning" to the new high school sport, baseball. For good measure, four Halstad players were pictured in a painfully staged pose "plotting strategy."

Media attention or not, Kerrigan was now in a deeper bind. He had nobody to pitch the championship game. Morrie Holm had thrown thirteen innings in two days. The scorebook, which doesn't show how many foul balls Morrie gave up on two strikes, shows that he threw 95 pitches the first night and approximately 80 pitches the second night. By modern standards his arm should have been mush.

Once again, Arnold Kittleson let down his decorum. He and Kerrigan, knowing that it would likely have to be Morrie pitching the final game against Austin, massaged his arm with ointments. They started with hot towels, then they switched to cold towels. Morrie felt honored—and bemused.

"I never figured I'd have the superintendent there holding my hand and rubbing my arm," he says today.

For Kerrigan, there was an ethical issue. Morrie was a promising pitcher. He had a future in college. What if Kerrigan ruined his arm by overusing him in a vain attempt to win a state title? Was a state title worth the risk to Morrie's future? To make matters worse, the championship game would be nine innings, not seven innings as had been all of the games in Halstad's season up to this point.

Kittleson and Kerrigan quizzed Morrie. How did his arm feel? Morrie wanted to pitch, and badly. As with most pitchers who want to pitch, coaches sometimes suspect they are being less than truthful about the state of their arm. Kittleson and Kerrigan finally believed what Morrie told them: His body was weary, but his arm didn't hurt.

After a fairly sleepy baseball season, Ray Kerrigan again found himself in the cauldron of media attention.

If he blew out Morrie's arm, he could be disgraced state-wide. Ray Kerrigan didn't sleep that night. Instead, he walked the streets of Owatonna smoking cigarette after cigarette.

The next morning, a Friday, it started to rain. It poured until about noon, and then backed off a bit. Dartt's Field was soggy. Tournament organizers announced that if the championship game could not be played, it would be moved to Saturday. One has to think that Ray Kerrigan was hoping for a postponement, if for no other reason than to give him some cover for his now inevitable decision to pitch Morrie Holm.

But the rain held off. To allow time for the field to be put into playing condition, the third-place game was canceled. Time and again, gasoline was poured over the infield and lit up in an effort to dry off the dampness. The championship game, which was originally scheduled for 8 p.m., didn't start until nearly ten o'clock in the evening. Over 580 people bought tickets for the game.

Austin was regarded as the best team in the tournament. They had a potent line-up, led by the Rasmussen twins, and they had an ace pitcher in Ron Plath. But Plath, who had been pulled out early in Austin's first game rout against tiny Bricelyn and who had pitched an inning of relief in Austin's semifinal win against St. Paul Monroe, was tired as well. The championship game would be an endurance contest. Who would soften first, Holm or Plath?

Morrie loaded the bases in the first inning but got out of the jam with a big strikeout. Plath allowed two Pirate runners in the first inning on a walk and an error, but got Dale Serum to ground out to second to end the threat. Both pitchers retired the side 1-2-3 in the second inning.

After George "Squirt" Johnson struck out to lead off the third, Hesby singled and Bernhagen doubled. Halstad had a threat going with one out, but Oien popped up to first base and Akason grounded out short to first. Still no score.

In the third inning, Morrie began to labor. After running up a full count, he walked the Austin leadoff hitter, who then went to second base on an error. Although he retired the next three batters, one on a strikeout, Morrie went to a full count on each of the batters. He was tired, and it was starting to show in his control.

Halstad went quietly in the fourth inning, as did Austin. After four innings of play, the game was scoreless. Plath and Morrie were locked in an old-fashioned pitcher's duel.

Then came the fifth. To get something started, Kerrigan began the inning by pinchhitting sophomore Don Lervold for light-hitting senior George Johnson. Lervold walked, as did Hesby. Now it was Plath's turn to show fatigue. Hesby and Lervold pulled off a double steal, and then Bernhagen filled the bases by coaxing the inning's third walk off Plath.

Wally Oien smashed the ball to the shortstop, who bobbled it, allowing Lervold to score the game's first run. Jimmy Akason drew the fourth walk of the inning, which forced in Darrel Hesby with Halstad's second run. Dale Serum then singled, which scored Bernhagen and Oien. The Pirates were breaking the game open, and there was nobody out in the inning.

Marlyn Aanenson struck out for the first out, but the next batter, second baseman Curt Johnson, hit into a fielder's choice, which scored Jimmy Akason for Halstad's fifth run. That was the end of the line for Ron Plath, who was replaced by Austin ninth-grade phenomenon Gary Underhill. Underhill, a left-hander, retired Morrie on a ground out and then faced little Donny Lervold, now batting for the second time in the inning. Lervold rapped a double to right-center field, which scored Serum and Curt Johnson. Lervold had scored 1 run in the inning and drove in 2, and the Pirates had opened up a 7-run lead.

The suspense built as everyone watched to see if Morrie could hang on. Between innings, Kerrigan had Wally Oien warming up on the sideline. But with a state championship in view, Kerrigan wanted to stick with his ace. Also between innings, Arnold Kittleson sat rubbing Morrie's arm with ointments.

Like Plath, Morrie faltered in the fifth. An error led off the inning, and the Halstad hurler walked two out of the next three hitters to load the bases with one out. Another error scored a run, and a hit by Dayle Rasmussen, the same Dayle Rasmussen who had scored 28 points against Halstad three months before at Williams Arena, brought in Austin's second run. Although Halstad had a big lead, Morrie was tired and was throwing a lot of pitches. And there were four more innings to go.

If Kerrigan would have had any other pitchers available, he would have put one in at this point. With a 5-run lead, it appeared the Morrie didn't have any gas left in his tank. But Kerrigan stuck with the tired right-hander, and Morrie kept pitching, taking his time, infuriating the radio announcers with his rituals, and one by one retiring the Austin batters.

After the Pirates added a run in the sixth, Morrie walked one batter but retired the other three. In the seventh, Halstad scored again in the top of the inning. In

the bottom, Morrie recorded two strikeouts, hit one batter, and got the third to ground out to Jimmy Akason at
shortstop.

Now the Pirates could smell a championship. They
led 9–2. Morrie wasn't going to leave the game. Kerrigan
wasn't of a mind to pull him. And so Morrie Holm reached
back and found something extra.

In a 1-2-3 eighth inning, he struck out two batters
and induced another to hit a fly ball to Hesby in center
field. The ninth started with another fly to Hesby. After
striking out the Austin leadoff hitter, an error allowed a
runner to reach first. On a one-ball, one-strike count,
Austin's batter lifted a fly ball to Hesby in center field.
Just as Hesby had ended the basketball season by sink-
ing a basket in sudden death against Austin at Williams
Arena, now Hesby ended Austin's baseball season by
catching the final out in Dartt's Park in Owatonna.

It was nearly midnight. The team and its coach
rushed onto the field and carried Morrie Holm off on their
shoulders. Kerrigan put his arm around his exhausted
pitcher. Photos in the next day's paper were captioned
"Coach Beams at Protégé." Hesby tried to get the game
ball for Morrie, but tournament officials insisted upon
taking it from him. The mother of Austin's Rasmussen

twins worked her way to Morrie and told him that while she wished her boys' team had won, Morrie's performance was deserving of the state title.

The sheriff was as excited as anybody. His buddies from Halstad, whom he had met three days earlier, had won him over as surely as they had won over Manny Marget three months earlier. Kerrigan and the sheriff became friends, and it was a shock to the 1952 players when Kerrigan informed them two years later that the big guy had died of a heart attack.

Once it became clear that the game would start very late, Arnold Kittleson had taken off to go uptown and convince a restaurant to stay open until after the game. The boys were exhausted and hungry. Thanks to Kittleson, they were treated to a midnight, postgame, celebratory steak dinner.

Almost single-handedly, Morrie Holm had won the state title for the Halstad Pirates. Although the Halstad team was solid and had a capable enough offense to take advantage of errors by the other teams, without Morrie, Halstad simply would not have stood a chance.

In an instant, Morrie Holm rose out of obscurity. The *Minneapolis Tribune* touted him as an "Iron Man Pitcher." And finally, Morrie got the credit he deserved for his tournament performance.

In the three-day tournament, Morrie Holm had pitched twenty-two of his team's twenty-three innings. In those twenty-two innings, he struck out 35 batters, including 13 of the hard-hitting Austin hitters. He pitched two complete games, a three-hitter and a two-hitter. Only errors in the field prevented Morrie from pitching two shutouts.

To those impressive statistics, add one more. In the modern day, great attention is paid to a pitcher's pitch count. Very seldom is a pitcher allowed to throw more than 120 pitches in a five-day span.

Against New Ulm in the first round of the tournament, Morrie registered approximately 95 pitches. In the second game the next night, he threw between 75 and 80 pitches. In two days, he threw more pitches than major league pitchers today are allowed to throw in a five-day span.

Then, on the third day, Morrie came back against Austin and pitched a nine-inning complete game. Because he was tired and somewhat wild, he gave up more walks than usual and took many other batters to full counts. By the end of the championship game, as the scorebook shows in Ray Kerrigan's faint handwriting, Morrie threw at least 145 pitches—before one considers the two strike foul balls which don't appear in the book.

It was an epic performance by the Halstad ace, and it would never be repeated. In response to Morrie's iron-man performance, the Minnesota State High School League immediately passed a rule limiting the number of innings any one pitcher could throw in a tournament.

There is no indication that Morrie ever developed arm troubles due to the innings he threw in the state tournament. He went on to a successful college career at North Dakota State University.

In his final year of college, Morrie received a contract in the mail from the Cleveland Indians. It said nothing about money, or where Morrie would play. He wasn't impressed. He stuck it in his top dresser drawer back at the farm. He was going to get married, and he was slated to enter the army that winter to fulfill his ROTC obligation. Playing professional ball probably wasn't in the cards. Morrie forgot about the contract.

"I suppose my sisters threw it away when they were getting ready for the auction," he says years later, with a shrug.

After the state tournament, Kerrigan told the press of his long-standing plans to retire from coaching. Larry

Macleod was ready to take over, and Kerrigan had enough on his plate as it was. Headlines in the *Minneapolis Tribune* heralded the retirement of the man who had led the Halstad wonder boys of 1952 to a third-place finish in the basketball tournament and a first-place finish in the state baseball tournament.

A tired Halstad team headed back home Saturday morning. The weather was a lot nicer than it had been when it took 10 hours to drive home three months before. Even so, Bake Johnson got lost. The players in his car missed out on the celebration.

It wasn't much of a celebration compared to the hoopla which surrounded the return of the basketball team, but it was enough. Sixty cars plus the Halstad fire truck greeted the team at Four Mile Corner, an intersection four miles south of town. At the intersection, the *Norman County Index* took photos, one of Morrie, looking very tired, and another of the entire team, minus Curt Johnson, Darrel Hesby, and Jimmy Akason, who were in Bake Johnson's car.

The team then drove ten miles into Ada where the Norman County Fair was in full swing. That evening's event at the fairgrounds was stopped while the cars of players drove in front of the grandstand to be introduced as the state baseball champions. Then the entire entourage drove back to Halstad. The cars in the processional were the first vehicles to use the new highway, recently renumbered Highway 75, which had just been paved. Although it wasn't open for general traffic yet, on this Saturday the procession skirted the barricades and drove the last four miles into Halstad on the perfectly smooth concrete surface.

Unlike the coverage of the basketball team, the Pirate baseball team was late in getting press. The *Fargo Forum* featured the team, as did the *Minneapolis Tribune*. An official of the Minnesota State High School League told the *Tribune* that Halstad's victory was the best thing that could have happened to the baseball tournament, which was in its beginning stages and still trying to distinguish itself from town baseball, American Legion baseball, and Jaycee baseball. In fact, the big newspapers paid little or no attention to the tournament until Morrie's "iron-man" performance.

It wasn't more than a few days before the boys who won the state title were back on the field for Erwin Warner's Halstad Red Sox. Morrie found out soon just how much slack his newfound fame would cut him with opposing fans. Erwin put Morrie on the mound against Nielsville, a tiny town just up Highway 75 which featured some beefy sluggers in the middle of their line-up. The Nielsville nine started pounding Morrie's offerings over the fence.

"Let's hear it for the famous Morrie Holm!" one Nielsville fan hollered.

"Why don't you throw 'em your clippings!" yelled another.

After a dramatic interlude in Owatonna, summer baseball was back to normal in Halstad.

In retirement, Larry Macleod pondered the Halstad Pirate baseball team of 1952. In his mid-eighties, Macleod didn't remember any particularly great hitters on the team. He said the Halstad defense was above average, but not spectacular, especially by modern standards. Dale Serum was an outstanding catcher, Marlyn Aanenson was a solid first baseman, and Wally Oien could fly in center field, but that was about it. No, Macleod said, there was really nothing which might have foretold that the Halstad Pirate team would walk through a state tournament stacked with teams from large schools from areas of the state where baseball was much bigger business than it was in the Red River Valley.

"But," Macleod said, as he scratched his chin, "we had Morrie."

Aftermath

After the 1952 season, Ray Kerrigan got job offers. There were feelers from big suburban schools, most notably from Bloomington, Minnesota. Some people from Thief River Falls contacted him informally about the basketball job there, although Bob Nick was eventually retained. Instead, Ray Kerrigan stuck to his decision to retire from coaching and turn the reins over to Larry Macleod. Kerrigan knew he wasn't enough of a nuts-and-bolts coach to enjoy the competition at a higher level. He knew as well that he owed a lot of his success as a coach in 1952 to an exceptional crop of athletes, a good assistant coach in Larry Macleod, and a lot of help from Erwin Warner. Kerrigan also knew that no amount of success at a larger school would match the fun of the 1952 season, when Halstad surprised so many around the state. Kerrigan was satisfied to teach, be principal, and bury himself in community affairs in Halstad.

Kerrigan's retirement from coaching lasted one year. Larry Macleod resigned and became the head men's basketball coach at Moorhead State Teachers College. Kerrigan returned to coaching for another six years. During those years, he had some very good teams. Each year, it seemed, Kerrigan would threaten to retire, only to return for the next season.

In 1956, led by ace scorer Alden Holte, Halstad won the district title, beat Crookston in opening round of the regional tournament, and lost to Bemidji in a last-second heartbreaker in the region final.

Led by Dale Olson in 1957, the Pirates reached the district final where they played the Mahnomen Indians. The Pirates fell behind by as many as 19 points in the second quarter, pulling to within 16 points by the half. In the locker room, Kerrigan was steamed.

"That's one hell of a way to end a career," he snorted, once again playing the retirement card before slamming his clipboard down and heading out for a smoke.

The somewhat self-pitying motivational speech worked. Halstad roared back from the 16-point deficit to overcome Mahnomen by 1 point in the final seconds. It was a stinging defeat for the Mahnomen Indians, who figured they had the superior team. The results didn't slow down Mahnomen Coach Lute Olson, a former Grand Forks Central star who later became one of the most successful coaches in NCAA history. Halstad, meanwhile, went on to lose the opening game of the regional tournament to defending champion Bemidji.

Of all of Ray Kerrigan's outstanding teams, nobody went further than the 1952 bunch. In Kerrigan's honor, an old-timers' basketball game was held in the Halstad gym in 1960. It pitted the 1952 team against the players from every other year combined. Darrel Hesby, of all the players, had kept his skills most honed. He scored well over 20 points, and the 1952 team won again.

The old-timers' game was held because in 1960, Ray Kerrigan retired from coaching for good. The Halstad high school had grown through consolidation to the point where it needed a full-time principal. Arnold Kittleson and Kerrigan made a good administrative team. Kittleson, the superintendent, took care of the business end and made sure the books were balanced to the penny, while Kerrigan, the principal, made sure everybody in school was disciplined, orderly, respectful, appropriate, and appreciated.

For the rest of his career, Kerrigan missed coaching, mainly because he no longer was as close to the boys on the team. They no longer hung out at the house. No more late-night gatherings after games to discuss what went right and what went wrong.

In the late 1960s, Kerrigan's old friend Erwin Warner, who was always stirring the pot over something, turned his energies towards ousting Arnold Kittleson from the superintendent job. Nobody to this day knows why.

Because Kerrigan was friends with both Kittleson and Erwin, he was in a bind. Kerrigan was the obvious choice to succeed Kittleson should Erwin's campaign succeed, and Kerrigan wanted nothing to do with the job if he took it at Arnold's expense.

Arnold called Kerrigan into his office and laid things out on the table. He was going to leave town. He had found a good job in a larger school in southern Minnesota and would be well taken care of. Kerrigan was to take the superintendent's job no matter how shady the reasons for its having come open. Kerrigan reluctantly agreed. It was sordid business, and the conditions of Kerrigan's rise to the superintendent position took all the joy out of the promotion.

Unlike Arnold Kittleson, Ray Kerrigan finished his career in Halstad. He wasn't a financial whiz like Kittleson, but he maintained his big smile and his charismatic presence. His mop of hair slowly grayed. Thanks to the success of the 1952 teams, Kerrigan was sort of a resident legend, and he loved to tell stories about that season.

In the summer of 1977, he decided to retire after one more year as superintendent. Before his last school year began, however, Kerrigan developed an aneurysm in his stomach. After weeks of battling the affliction, Kerrigan died in August at the age of 60.

With the exception of Chuck Bernhagen, who returned to Bird Island, the careers of the players—the Starting Five and others who were under Kerrigan's tutelage for three or four years—bear upon them the unmistakable stamp of Ray Kerrigan. Thompson, Hesby, Aanenson, Akason, Holm, and Serum all played sports in college. Don Thompson became a teacher and coached. Darrel Hesby became a teacher and coached. Jim Akason became a teacher and coached. Morrie Holm studied to become a teacher, then became an agriculture extension agent. Dale Serum became an athletic director.

Don Thompson married his sweetheart Jane Jorgenson from Halstad. Darrel Hesby married his sweetheart Janet Sulerud from Halstad. Dale Serum married his sweetheart Carol Henderson from Halstad. Morrie Holm married Wally Oien's sister Maxine from Halstad. Of the Starting Five, only Jim Akason strayed from Halstad to find a wife. Carol Svendson was from Shelly, five miles to the north.

And, to quote a proud Larry Macleod fifty-five years later, "there hasn't been one divorce in the bunch."

All the players had children, many of whom excelled in athletics. Jim Akason's son scored 1,000 points in his career, making the Akasons for some time the only father-son combination to each reach that benchmark. Dale Serum's boy Gary pitched for the Minnesota Twins. Darrel Hesby's grandchildren excel at hockey.

Now in their early seventies, the players are still active, mostly in golf—except for Darrel Hesby, who can't stand the sport. Instead, Hesby continues to play competitive basketball three days per week with people less than half his age. With the three-point rule, Hesby's long shots are even more valuable on the court than they were in 1952. With his 29-inch waist and his full head of hair which shows no hint of gray, Hesby still has the ability to taunt his peers, now without even opening his mouth.

Don and Jane Thompson keep busy with grandchildren and building ornate, scale-model doll houses, at least a dozen of which are on display in the basement of their spacious Mahnomen home. Morrie Holm lives with Maxine in Lakota, North Dakota. In retirement, he spearheaded the building of a golf course on the edge of town. Dale Serum plays a lot of golf and spends winters with Carol at a mobile home park in Arizona. Jim Akason lives right on a golf course in Sun City West with Carol.

Good, solid people with good, solid careers—but not a one of them stayed in Halstad. In fact, only one member of the entire 1952 basketball team spent his life in

Halstad, and that was underclassman Bobby Olson who farmed east of town. Marlyn Aanenson went into teaching before landing an accounting job in Fargo. George Allen "Squirt" Johnson became a professor of business in Idaho. Frankie Steenerson worked for Boeing in Seattle.

"Nobody ever said, 'Son, you've got to get out of town,'" Jim Akason says today, "but it was clear early on that there was no future for me there."

Despite the liveliness of Halstad in the early 1950s, the Starting Five, unlike their parents, hadn't even a notion that they could stay in Halstad, raise a family, and make a decent living. Darrel Hesby knew from an early age that pumping fuel in Halstad like his father wasn't what he wanted to do for a living. Morrie Holm's father didn't have enough land to divide among even two children, much less eleven. In fact, the Holm farm would need to multiply in size to support even one family. Dale Serum had no desire to build houses for an hourly wage as his father did. Don Thompson wasn't about to take over his father Leonard's position as a farm laborer on Bennitt Aarestad's potato farm. None of the Starting Five came from privilege. None of them stepped into a business or farm situation created by their parents. They all struck out on their own.

Striking out on one's own meant something different for the generation that came of age in 1952 than it had meant for any previous generation. Unlike their immediate elders, the Starting Five didn't have a world war to fight. They didn't have a Great Depression to struggle through. They didn't have land to clear for crops. They didn't have to learn a new language and acclimate to a new culture as had their grandparents. In fact, the Starting Five were part of the first generation on the farm that had no obvious, pressing tasks foisted upon them at the onset of adulthood.

But they did have opportunities. They knew that they could go to college. Ten years before, the idea of non-academically-inclined males going to college to figure out what they wanted to do with their lives would have seemed absurd. By 1952, however, a lot had changed on the higher-education front. The GI Bill had resulted in thousands of returning veterans attending college. For the first time in American history, males went to college in mass numbers.

The 1952 Starting Five had several examples in front of their noses: Their assistant coach, Larry Macleod, had gone to college on the GI Bill, which he calls today, "A wonderful, wonderful piece of legislation."

Other veterans from Halstad were in college and came home in the summers to play ball or to work. Ray Kerrigan was college educated. Rev. Carl Opsahl was obviously a man of letters. And for all his crudeness, even Erwin Warner understood the need for a college education enough to support at least one Halstad student financially. These weren't effete intellectual snobs. They were the men the kids looked up to, the men who had led them into battle on the court and ball diamond. And these men valued higher education. No wonder almost everybody on the 1952 team ended up in college, whether they went there to play ball or not.

Today, Jim Akason still lauds the GI Bill, even though it didn't aid him one bit financially: "We saw all these guys going to college, and we said, 'Hey, maybe that's what I want to do.'" The examples provided by Macleod, Kerrigan, Opsahl, and other returning vets in Halstad made a difference.

The importance of Kerrigan, Macleod, Erwin, and Opsahl as role models brings up another question: Where were all these boys' fathers? Busy making a living, of course. But there was more to it than that. Fathers of the time were expected to be distant. Before the war, their role had been to prepare their sons for work on the farm. As farming mechanized, however, the sons spent more time at school under the tutelage of education professionals—teachers and coaches. It took awhile, at least a generation, for fathers to adjust and realize that if they wanted to get to know their sons at all, they had better take an interest in their schooling and sports activities.

Many old-timers lament the demise of the old 1950s ethic whereby the teacher was always right, the pastor was always right, the superintendent was always right, and if the kid got in trouble at school or at confirmation class, he was in even more trouble at home. Today, goes the argument, pampered kids can do no wrong in the eyes of their parents, while teachers, it seems, can do no right. Kids in trouble can rely on their parents to defend them and help them wriggle off the hook.

The real picture is probably more complex. Parents in the 1950s were quite distant, even deliberately so. Martin Akason's interest in Jimmy Akason's basketball career was the exception and not the rule, and it didn't necessarily translate into coziness.

Adding to the distance between parents and children in Halstad was the stoic Scandinavian culture. Norwegian parents didn't often brim with affection. It seems that there was a very real fear, particularly in the fathers, of being too soft on the boys, of not preparing them for the rough-and-tumble world. As a result, relations between sons and fathers were more stilted and formal than they are today.

"I didn't ever really talk to my dad until he got in the nursing home," is a common refrain.

"I really wish I had asked him about some of that stuff," the sons say today when they are asked about their fathers' war experiences or early farming experiences or whatever they might have done in the old days.

Into this somewhat cold parental situation stepped Ray Kerrigan, an Irishman who came from a family headed by a gregarious and fun-loving father with whom he got along well. Kerrigan had no fear of friendships with his players, no sense that his dignity would be compromised by joking with them, talking to them, patting them on the back, kicking them on the butt, swearing at them, laughing with them, and celebrating with them. He was free with his advice, relaxed, and himself at all times.

Then there was Erwin Warner. For all his crudeness, many players say that he was a father figure to them. Erwin treated the players as sons, gave them jobs on his farm, cooked them bacon and eggs for breakfast, let them pump gas out of his farm tank, swore with them, told them dirty stories, and taught them baseball.

At the opposite pole, but with the same goal in mind, was Rev. Carl Opsahl. Although a paragon of virtue, Opsahl wasn't as stern as he seemed. Kids were comfortable with him. He and Mrs. Opsahl expressed their interest in the kids through Luther League. Frequently, they took several young people, including Don Thompson, to the national Luther League convention, even when it was as far away as Seattle.

The interest of these adults in the community's kids stood in contrast to the attitude of the parents, many of whom hadn't figured out how to be a part of their children's lives, or even saw the need. So, it is possible that the "teacher is always right" ethic was more a "leave it to the professionals" attitude. The teachers, coaches, principals, and ministers are the people we hire to train our kids; they need the power to do their job. So good grief, kids, don't screw things up so your parents have to leave their busy lives to come in and visit with the principal.

Even with distant parents, though, the early 1950s were a gem of a time to grow up. Yet none of the Starting Five stayed in Halstad. Like every small farm town on the prairie, Halstad was changing fast and in big ways.

In late 1953, the first television signal reached Halstad from WDAY in Fargo. The introduction of television probably altered the small town social fabric more than anything. Before television, the excuse given for the constant buzz of community activity was, "We were desperate for something to do." With television, there was always something to do. The newest electronic diversion came with a flip of a switch and didn't require dealing with people.

Basketball kept up its remarkable popularity for at least a decade. The Minnesota State Basketball Tournament reached its peak in 1960 when little Edgerton, the darling of all tournament darlings, won the state tournament at Williams Arena. From then on, however, things went downhill. The teams were split up into classes by school size, first into two classes, then into four. In the interests of allowing more kids to participate in the state tournaments, the possibility of a darling like Halstad dominating the state news media ended.

Plus, there were other high school sports competing for fans. Wrestling became popular. Hockey continued to grow. Girls basketball started again in the mid-1970s, and thanks to some excellent players such as Janet Karvonen of New York Mills, the game became an instant hit. When the Minnesota State High School League tried to revive some of the old magic of the State Boys Basketball Tournament in the mid-1990s by combining the state tournament into one class with sixteen entrants, it failed. The stands at the various arenas were half-empty, even for championship games. The Old Barn, Williams Arena, which had been a part of the state tournament mystique of the 1950s, was remodeled and split down the middle, with one side used for Minnesota Gopher basketball and the other for hockey.

Town baseball also started to decline immediately after 1952, just after nearly every small town in Minnesota had put up lights around its field. When the Washington Senators moved to Minnesota to become the Twins in 1961, town baseball suffered its biggest blow. Crowds dwindled. Teams folded due to lack of interest. Fields grew up in grass.

Due to declining enrollment, consolidation of schools continued beyond the boundaries of individual towns. It usually started with athletic pairings. Halstad paired with Hendrum for some sports in hopes of fielding a more competitive team, as well as to save money on coaches and facilities. As one Hendrum basketball fan put it, "I thought it would be a cold day in hell before I sat on the same side of the gym as Wally Oien." But there he was in 1982, cheering for a new creation, the Panthers. The Halstad Pirates had played their last game.

Eventually, the Hendrum and Halstad schools would combine into Norman County West. Under Erwin Warner's boy, Cactus, the Norman County West basketball team won the Class A basketball title in 1982, but the hoopla didn't match the third-place finish of the old Halstad Pirates in 1952.

With the constant changes, the blood drained from the old rivalries. People have an inbred need to pull for a team, to jump on a bandwagon, to be a part of a successful athletic endeavor, even if only vicariously. But the energy for being a fan is limited, and rare is the person who can divide his or her loyalties ten ways without diminishing the intensity of devotion to one team in particular. In 1952, there was one outlet for the collective booster energies of Halstadites, and that was their basketball team. In 2007, there are the Norman County West teams, of course, but there are also the Minnesota Twins, the Minnesota Gophers, the Minnesota Wild, the Minnesota Vikings, the Fargo-Moorhead Redhawks, any one of which could be playing on satellite television as we speak. People tend to become fans of the biggest, most successful team around. Sports fans are going to choose the Minnesota Twins, who they can watch every evening all summer, over the Norman County West Panthers—unless they have a child or grandchild actually playing for the Panther team.

The changes in schools and high school athletics pale in comparison to the larger changes which have hit Halstad and every other small town on the prairie. The number one change, the one that has propelled so much other change, is the increased size of farms. Family farms went from a couple of hundred acres to many thousands. Some turned corporate and got bigger yet.

In the U.S.S.R, Joseph Stalin killed millions to communalize agriculture, to turn the patchwork little plots of old into massive, efficient fields. In the Red River Valley, much the same result was achieved through a combination of the free market and government policy. The tiny old farms have vanished, and the massive fields in their place leave no clue that for every square mile of sugar beets in perfect rows, there once were a half-dozen farmyards strewn with children, kittens, dogs, pigs, cows, horses, buggies, Model A's, spinster aunts, musty granaries, barns, and chicken coops.

Halstad, and the hundreds of small prairie towns like it, existed to serve the farms and the farm families. As farms increased in size, the need for the services in the small towns decreased. As the highways to larger towns improved, those people who did remain could easily travel to where they might find their groceries or hardware goods much cheaper. In Halstad's case, Fargo-Moorhead is forty miles to the south with its malls, discount stores, restaurants, car dealers, machinery dealers, and movie theaters.

Today, Halstad is lucky in that it remains the head-quarters for the regional telephone co-operative, as well as the regional electric co-operative. Otherwise, the town's main employers are the grain elevator, the nursing home, and the school.

When the Halstad Pirates went to the state tourna-ment in 1952, it was noted in the *Valley Journal* that 200 former Halstad residents lived in the Twin Cities alone. Hundreds of others had moved to the West Coast. Halstad, like all small towns on the prairie, was a nursery for the ballooning suburbs.

By the mid-1960s, Halstad's population started to age. The ability to replace the population that had gone to the city for jobs diminished. The John Wimmer retirement homes were built on the south edge of town. A nurs-ing home was built on the east edge of town in the late 1970s. Eventually, assisted-living facilities were added. As in many rural towns, caring for the elderly became an important industry and source of employment. By the

1980s, the death rate had surpassed the birth rate.

The bottom line is sobering. Halstad, like most towns of its size on the prairie, has lost its original reason to exist. The gathering of buildings on the prairie called Halstad is there simply as a relic of an earlier time. It is a nice place to live. It is quiet. There are no stoplights. Halstad Lutheran is still on its feet. Children can still run free. But the town is no longer a viable economic unit. As a result, Grandma Hesby's boarding house isn't the only building in Halstad which stands empty.

Today in Halstad there is one grocery store, one restaurant, one bank, no car dealers, one funeral home (another small-town necessity), one nursing home, one gas station, one hardware store, one print shop, and several beauty shops. The Sons of Norway site is now a vacant lot. The Woodman Theater has been replaced by an apartment building.

The town's lawns are mowed, even vacant buildings are kept in reasonably good shape, and the town still has a cozy feel. You can buy fresh pizza at the Cenex station, where you can also rent a movie, two things you couldn't do in 1952. You can get 400 channels of television, and high-speed Internet access is cheap from the local phone company.

But the baseball field is gone. The lights were eventually taken down. On a Saturday night, there might be a dozen cars parked outside the bar. And no matter how many games the consolidated Norman County West basketball team wins, you'll have no trouble whatsoever getting tickets.

In the summer of 2007, I stopped at the Lutheran Memorial Home in Halstad to visit with old Harris Henderson. Then I walked down the hall where a circle of ladies in wheelchairs were digesting their supper. Jeannette Enger told me her story about sharing a ticket with her dad at the Thief River Falls game. Others recalled their relatives driving up from Minneapolis to see a game. Everybody remembered the names of the Starting Five. Jimmy Akason. Darrel Hesby. Morrie Holm. Dale Serum. Don Thompson.

Things have changed in Halstad, all right. But, is it tragic?

Not to the kids who skateboard up and down the empty streets of Halstad on a warm summer's evening. Nor to the few young families who commute to jobs in Fargo, but who relish the quiet of the small town. Or to the residents of the nursing home who get some of the best care in the country. Or to the big farmers who race across the fields in their $350,000 combines, covering more territory in one day than farmers once did in an entire year.

In fact, the quiet of the small prairie towns is so attractive that some people are actually moving there to raise kids. Real estate prices have gone from abysmal to merely depressed. No longer can you buy an old house like the one Jimmy Akason or Don Thompson grew up in for $15,000 and fix it up. There is a growing sense in the small towns that after 100 years of steady decline, things are looking up.

Yet, no matter how much small-town life may improve, some things will never happen again. There is not going to be another Starting Five—young men who took their bustling little town for an unforgettable ride and who became larger-than-life heroes, even to people who saw them every day.

"People think you guys are above the earth," wrote Mrs. Thompson to her son Don while he was at the 1952 state basketball tournament.

"These guys walked on water," Clarence Stennes said as he introduced the men to me fifty-three years later.

No wonder the Starting Five who gathered in Cora Stennes' living room in July of 2005 sat with such dignified confidence as they waited for yet another press conference to begin. They had lived the dream of any small-town boy. They had taken their little town to the top.

The thrill hadn't worn off yet.

About the Author

Eric Bergeson is the third generation owner of Bergeson Nursery in Fertile, MN, a business started by his grandfather in 1937. He also writes a weekly column for several newspapers in northwestern Minnesota. He has published three books.

Eric graduated from Fertile-Beltrami High School in 1982. He attended Northwestern College in Roseville, MN, and received his bachelor's degree in history from the University of North Dakota in 1986. After completing a Bachelor of Science in Social Studies at Moorhead State University in 1988, he went back to UND where he earned a master's degree in history.

During college, Eric studied at Cambridge University in England, student taught in Wellington, NZ, and studied in Warsaw, Poland.

Eric is a frequent speaker and performer in northwestern Minnesota. Last year, he spoke or performed before over 40 clubs, groups, or community gatherings, usually, but not always, about gardening. He does radio shows on gardening over four area stations each spring. Eric and his brother Joe often sing and play piano for customers at the nursery, as well as for nursing homes and other community groups.

When needed, Eric teaches American history courses at the University of Minnesota, Crookston.

About the Sponsor

Clarence Stennes is a Halstad native who graduated from Halstad High School in 1959. After high school, he graduated from Concordia College in Moorhead, Minnesota, with a degree in economics and political science. In 1966 he obtained a graduate degree in economics from The University of Iowa and taught economics at Western Michigan University in Kalamazoo and at Simpson College in Indianola, Iowa. He received a law degree from Drake University in Des Moines, Iowa, and practiced law for twenty years. He and his wife, Barbara, live in Des Moines, Iowa. They are the parents of two grown children, Bryan and Erika.

Index

A

B

C

G

H

K

L

M

R

S

T

U

Ueland, Erman xiv, 99

Underhill, Gary 285

United States Naval Academy in Annapolis 184

University

of Arizona 161

of Iowa 318

of Minnesota 6, 42, 190, 220, 228, 230, 318

of North Dakota 42, 184, 317

of Wisconsin 202

V

Valley Journal 51, 106, 122, 189, 198, 203, 239-40, 311

Viker, D.E. 189

Viker, Paul xiv

Viker, Rita xiv

Virginia 211-3, 215-9, 221-2, 224-5, 235, 240

W

Waite, Nancy 181

Wang, Bucky xiv

Warner, Erwin xii, 65, 84, 101, 106, 112, 120-1, 126, 140, 164, 166, 168, 206, 235, 244-54, 256-8, 260, 262, 264-5, 268, 270, 274, 281, 295, 298, 303, 305, 309

Warroad 248-9

Waubun Bombers 116

WDAY 88, 92, 109-10, 306

Weaver, Bill 92, 109

Western Michigan University in Kalamazoo 318

Whoopee John's Orchestra 59

Williams Arena 6, 85, 120, 190-4, 197, 203-4, 207, 212-4, 222, 227-8, 234, 266, 281, 286-7, 307-8

Williams, Ted vi, 74

Williamson, Allan xiv, 186-7